GROUSE, QUAIL AND A *SPLASH* OF WOODCOCK

By Frank Jezioro

Foreword by Dave Meisner

ISBN 0-9665611-0-4

Library of Congress 98-091654

Published by
LARSEN'S OUTDOOR PUBLISHING

Distributed by

OLD DRUMMER'S KENNEL
Rt. #1, Box 183-A
Flemington, WV 26347

PRINTED IN THE UNITED STATES OF AMERICA

1 2 3 4 5 6 7 8 9 10

DEDICATION

To my grandfather who took me in at age three, raised me as a son and taught me to hunt.

To my children who never questioned my passion for hunting and dogs, but instead became a loving and willing part of it. And especially to Beverly who has become my favorite hunting buddy, and to George, "Pops" Burroughs, more family than friend, who thought he saw a small diamond sparkling under a pile of Appalachian coal. If I sparkle at all it is because of the faith and support of George. Thank you all, and to all of you this book is dedicated.

ACKNOWLEDGMENT

Parts of two stories in this book have appeared in Pointing Dog Journal and parts of others may appear in the future. I must thank Pointing Dog Journal's Editor-Publisher, Dave Meisner for his patience and support during the infancy of my writing career.

I also thank fellow West Virginian, George Bird Evans for writing the Upland Shooting Life which I consider one of the two best books ever written to convey the feelings of those of us who follow the dogs with a shotgun. George's writing was a great inspiration when I sat down to express my own feelings for the dogs the guns and the men who owned them.

And thanks also to Corey Ford, whose Tinkhamtown burned lasting impressions into my own mind, and to Randy Lawrence who met the challenge of my mentor George Burroughs by taking me through a long distance correspondence course of creative writing. Sometimes we agreed and sometimes we didn't, but I am stronger for his guidance. All of you must accept credit, or maybe blame, for the writing of this book.

FOREWORD

Grouse, Quail And A *Splash* of Woodcock

The thunderous roar of a ruffed grouse as it bursts from beneath a blowdown, the heart-stopping rise of a covey of bobwhites on the edge of a stubble field, a longbill, pinned under a stiff-as-stone point by a promising young prospect — these are things the shooting man lives for, the things that keep us coming back, things Frank Jezioro knows well.

I would venture to say that I've read a thousand manuscripts that have been submitted to me by freelance writers on the subject of hunting grouse, quail, or woodcock. With that kind of reading experience, and having gunned these birds extensively myself, it usually doesn't take more than a paragraph or two to determine whether or not the writer knows of which he writes. Many don't, but Frank's writings ring true. You know he's really been here.

In another foreword to another book, I wrote that there is an enormous difference between a writer who occasionally happens to hunt, and a hunter who happens to write. Today's general interest outdoor magazines, and many books, are filled with drivel by the former. Frank, on the other hand, is first and foremost a hunter who—fortunately for the rest of us — can write, and who enjoys sharing his gunning experiences with others.

The truly serious upland gunner is a dog man — let there be no mistake of that. Memories of birds, and locations, and the shots made or missed fade with time, but spectacular dog work — a pup's first point a on wild bird, the powerful performance of a young dog coming into its prime, and incredible retrieve — these things live on as our temples gray and the cut of our wrinkles grow deeper. And thus you will find the names of Tomba and

Pixie, and a few others, liberally sprinkled throughout this volume, for Frank knows dogs too, and their integral role in our lives as upland gunners.

In the pages that follow, you will find Tomba hard on point, with Pixie backing — or maybe the other way around — and you'll learn from a hunter who writes, from the heart, the joy of being afield with gun and dog.

Dave Meisner, Publisher and Editor-in-Chief
The Pointing Dog Journal
Adel, Iowa
February, 1997

PREFACE

"Grouse, Quail And A *Splash* of Woodcock" is a Companion to "Of Guns and Dogs and Men"

Here Frank will share with the readers his ongoing journey through a life so intertwined with this thing we call Bird hunting. Across the world, the Good Lord sprinkled a few unique individuals who were destined to be bird hunters. They are driven by a deep passion to follow the dogs. For the bird hunter there is no open or closed season. Instead his or her life is in a constant state of progression from one stage to another which just happen to coincide with the opening of this or that season.

The true bird hunters are individuals who will chance a crash, swerving their $35,000.00 Range Rover to miss a mother and her brood of young grouse only to return three months later to relentlessly pursue them with the dogs, a good shotgun and an insatiable passion.

The true bird hunters plan all the major events in their lives around the hunting seasons. They schedule weddings, christenings, graduations, vacations and, sometimes, even deaths around the opening of some bird season around the country.

Frank has been described as a writer with that natural gift of being able to place the reader beside him as he walks the covets from the Southern Appalachians, up through the Lake States, across the Heartland and on into Canada where he and the dogs hunt grouse, quail and woodcock.

Walking with him through this book you will hear, and feel, the wind and the wings, smell the powder, the bogs and the wet dogs, and see the colors of fall, as only a bird hunter sees them. Follow along with Frank, side by side, watching those magnificent dogs scour the upland swales that open before you. If you love the dogs, the birds, the guns, the hunters and the country, come, walk with Frank.

For you individuals, young and not so young alike, who live for those cherished moments when you can follow your dogs with a good gun, this book was written.

CONTENTS

CHAPTER 1

COVERTS FOUND AND LOST

There Is a Tinkhamtown

There are two important things I have told my children to ask of any would-be spouse. First they are to ask if the would-be spouse's family owns any large amounts of land where their poor old father might pass his remaining years following his bird dogs. Second they are to ask if they know where there are any grouse. After those questions are satisfied, the remaining ones may or may not be of any importance. Now that I reflect back to my own youth I realize this was the way I started most conversations with people to whom I was introduced.

And so it was that I opened a conversation once with an old mountaineer over in Upshur County, WV. I had to see the fellow on company business. I was working as a claims adjuster for a large auto insurance company at the time. One of our insureds had his head buried in a Jack Daniels bottle and stuck his 4X4 pickup into this old man's kitchen around midnight one night. Looking back I remember that the first thing I saw as I pulled into the yard was the large expanse of grouse cover that ran to the horizon of the mountain across the creek behind the old man's house. I don't think it had the slightest bearing on how the old fellow's claim was finally settled.

Anyway, after he had received a new porch, roof and siding on his house, he turned and pointed across the creek to where he said the pheasants (which was what most old timers in the area called grouse) were thick and that I could hunt to my heart's content as he owned the land as far as one could see. I liked this old man. He was sincere, and it was obvious that he had a true love and understanding of the land. He said that he really didn't own the land in the true sense of the word. He said that God had put it in his charge and that he was to take care of it and share its joys and bounties with the rest of mankind.

It was early May but I marked the spot well on my grouse map. I would return in late November and follow the remains of the old road that the farmer said would take me to the grouse. Things have changed now. During those early years of youth it seemed months were 60 and 80 days long. Now they appear only as glimpses, flickers or blinks of an eye. Now there are days that I stop to ponder *what is* from what *I wish it were.*

As it always has, November finally rolled around, and on one particularly crisp and sunny day I found myself headed from French Creek to Abbott. About half way I stopped at the house to tell the old man I was there.

In the short period since my last visit, he had gone. His wife told me it was sudden and that he only lasted a few days. That didn't surprise me nearly as much as when she told me that he had mentioned me during those last days. She said they had no children and he gave her specific instructions on what to do with the land when he was gone, and when it appeared she would follow. In all of his final instructions he had mentioned me. She said that he told her to let me hunt when I came back. She told me that she pointed out to him that I would probably never be back. To this he smiled and said only "oh, he will be back. When he comes you tell him follow to the road until it disappears in the thicket. Then bear left, up over the ridge and go deep into the next hollow. Tell him that's where he will find the pheasants."

I thanked her and set off across the creek with my young English setter. While I was in the house the clear sky had picked up a few lead-colored clouds and the air had switched from the west to the north. I remember thinking it seemed too early to snow but they sure looked like snow clouds. I was hunting Sally, a little tricolored setter and one of the great grouse dogs that I have been blessed to own and hunt behind. Together we found the remains of the old road and followed it through fields now going back to young brush and timber. I walked the old road while Sally swung right and left ahead of me.

Four hundred yards from the house the old road vanished without a trace, ending in a small clearing with only a few deer paths exiting the far side. I remembered that I was to bear left and headed off in that direction. The vegetation got much thicker and the going was actually tough. Briers and vines, as well as some pole sized young growth, stretched to the top of the ridge. The dog was cutting back and forth and checking as if to see if I was coming. She wasn't hunting but appeared to be headed somewhere and simply going through the motions as she searched.

Tomba, our present English setter, has all the qualities we want in an Appalachian grouse dog. He can hunt the mountains all day!

Just as we neared the top I stopped for a moment to get my breath. Sally swung by me and brushed my leg before heading on up the ridge. It was as if she were saying come on, let's go. Starting off again I hadn't gone 25 yards when I saw Sally frozen in her tracks. She was looking into a small patch of low pines. They were thick, and laced all through them were the hard, shiny greenbrier berries. Swinging out to the right I made my way back to the dog in a quartering movement, trying to pin the bird between us.

This close to the top I knew the bird would probably pitch over the ridge and into the next hollow. Nothing stirred as I eased into position. I saw Sally roll her eyes in my direction when I stepped on a small twig. I remember thinking that if I could get to that little dead chestnut snag, on the right there by the gray rock, I would be in good position. Another step or two and the pines exploded.

The first grouse caught me a little off balance and I shot behind as it bored past me headed for the next hollow over the ridge. I still had the gun up when the next one came out, only it wasn't one, it was three! Two thundered out after the first and the third spiraled to go up over the brush. I was swinging when he cleared the tops, and as he leveled off, a load of 7 1/2's from the imp. cyl. barrel hit him hard. He folded, dead in the air, coming down in a shower of leaves and small twigs.

Before he hit the ground I was aware of more wings and more flushes as grouse poured out of the tangle before me. Other than the one I shot they were all headed the same direction, over the ridge and into the next hollow. I fumbled with more shells as the ejectors kicked out the two spent ones, but I couldn't seem to load quickly enough as the birds sailed out in singles and pairs before the last one left and silence returned to the ridge top. Sally delivered the one bird I shot, and I looked around trying to recall what had just happened. I sat on an old log, turning to see if maybe someone else might be there to verify what I had just seen, but only Sally stood in front of me, staring into my face.

I asked Sally how many grouse there were, but she only looked deeper into my eyes. It seemed as if I was in the middle of a small tornado swirling around me, and spitting out grouse every time I turned. I wanted to load and shoot but my fingers had turned to lead bananas. Fluttering, brown wings were everywhere. It was as if I were on the outside, watching myself move about in slow motion as the grouse were blowing out in all directions, only to regroup and leave the clearing by the same path. As near as I could count there were somewhere from 12 to 15 different grouse that flew from that tangle in front of me.

The wind was getting stronger as we crossed the ridge. The clouds seemed lower and darker, and I couldn't see the bottom of the hollow as we started down to where the grouse had gone. Searching the head of the hollow for 30 minutes without a trace of a bird, not even a false point, I was starting to wonder if they hadn't cut left or right, going over the ridge and out of the hollow.

The cover was thin, old and uninviting as we headed on down towards the bottom. In a while I saw the tops of pines sticking up through the mixed hardwoods, and after another 100 yards we came out into an immense valley. The pines were scattered around traces of what appeared to be the remains of another old homestead. Looking around I soon found where the cellar house had stood as well as where the hand-dug well had been, long ago filled with debris.

Down the valley, we entered into as pretty a piece of grouse cover as I had ever seen. Like so many gray gnarled skeletons, ancient apple trees stood guard over the head of the long, narrow hollow. Woven through the trees were miles of grapevine and greenbrier. On the edges of what had once been fields were stands of sumac and clumps of multiflora rose.

It was as if someone had gone before me and planted what a grouse hunter considered ideal cover. I couldn't help but think of the soft, gentle smile of the old man, as he stood on his back porch pointing the way for me with a thin, weathered finger permanently bent from hours spent curled around a hoe and a scythe. I could hear him as I stood there alone and frozen in the moment "It is a long walk, but if you go over the far ridge and deep into the next valley you will find the pheasants. My father and I shot them along the tote road 70 years ago."

A sudden gust of cold wind brought me back to the moment at hand. My God, I was standing in the middle of Tinkhamtown! I called Sally in to my side and sat down for a moment to soak in all that surrounded me. I recalled all I could of that wonderful story written by Cory Ford, so many long years ago. When I read it back then, and Cory talked about finding Heaven, I was overwhelmed by what I thought was a wonderful, fictional story. Even when I was young I had my own picture of what heaven would be like for the bird hunter.

I had no desire to float around for eternity on a small white cloud with a golden harp in my hands. Heaven to the bird hunter would be an old road through an eternity of grouse cover that he and his never-aging dog could walk through while he carried a fine double shotgun. The dog would point every bird, and the hunter would kill it, only to hold it for a moments admiration before releasing it to fly again and again. This had to be what Cory was trying to tell us about.

It was 3:30 P.M. now and I was a good hour of hard walking from the car. I turned to whistle for Sally but there was no need. Not 50 yards away shc stood guarding a patch of sumac. So low and intense, I knew she had birds. I moved to my left and eased into the wind that was filling her nose with grouse. Three steps past her nose and the grouse burst from the tangle, hooking to my right.

Just as it cleared the trees I caught up with it and jerked the front trigger of the little Parker. Hit hard with a load of 7 1/2's, the bird crashed to the ground and fluttered a few times before Sally scooped it up and headed back to me. Like the others that lead me over the ridge, this grouse appeared to be as big as a Rhode Island Red chicken. I thought they must all be birds that were two or three years old. From the way they held for the dog I had the feeling they had never been hunted.

With the second bird tucked into the game bag I weaved my way on down the valley. Sally was on my right hitting some beautiful cover along the edge of the bank. I stopped to better enjoy the picture of her flowing over the ground. When I took the next step a grouse got up almost under my feet. I swung the gun on him just as he disappeared around the contour of the hill. Lowering the gun I took another step and two more grouse erupted from the bank above me and headed back towards the old foundation.

I began to experience the panic of youth, the panic you go through when you realize there are grouse all around you and they are all getting away. I didn't hear Sally's bell and stopped to whistle for her. She didn't come in and I hurried over to the hillside on my right where I had last seen her. Searching the thick cover I saw her tail first. She was looking at the base of one of the ancient apple trees.

I wanted to kill this bird. I don't know why it seemed so important but it did. I felt my hands tighten on the wrist of the Parker until my knuckles turned white. Rushing directly into the dog from her rear, I felt I had to get in front of her quickly. I never made it. Tangled up in a vine I stumbled, fought to regain my balance and heard the whir of wings. Not one pair, but three, taking off only seconds apart.

Sally broke and I didn't even stop to figure where they went. I seemed to be driven to plunge deeper and deeper into the valley ahead that fanned out in all directions. Not 75 yards further I came on Sally again. This time she was looking directly into the bank above her. This bird would have a tough time if he decided to hold. And hold he did. I was up to the dog now and staring into the bank not 10 feet away. Looking as hard as I could I didn't see anything, but Sally never flexed a hair. She knew he was there.

I started to the steep bank expecting a roar of wings at each step, my muscles so tight it was difficult to take the next step. There was one small

Early season gunning in the Appalachian Mountains is often done during rain and fog if you hunt the high country. Here, Tomba and the author take a moment to admire the first grouse of the West Virginia season.

autumn olive bush against the bank and I just knew the bird was behind it even though I couldn't see it. I bent to sort of peer around the bush. When I did I was looking into the big, brown eye of a grouse. It exploded in my face and roared back over my head. Turning in a frenzy I shot the first barrel before the gun ever reached my shoulder. The second one went off as the gun touched my shoulder but before I ever got on the bird.

At that moment I again felt this sense of urgency, this sense of having to hurry even though I seemed to be going through the cover at a run. I seemed late for something but had no idea what. Then a little voice within spoke to me. What's the hurry, where are you going? Slow down, take a look at what you have found here.

I called Sally in and I sat down on a huge, hand-cut stone. With Sally at my knee I rubbed her long soft ears and looked around. "Sally, we are in the middle of a grouse hunter's heaven," I told her. "There are birds everywhere and holding tight. We have killed two and you are doing a terrific job of finding and pointing one after another. The cover was as beautiful as any artist could paint it and we appear to be the only ones to have been here in years."

A sense of tranquillity came over me and I was no longer a man possessed. I came to realize this was what most grouse hunters search a lifetime for. We had stepped back into another time, a time of big, handsome, square-headed, tricolored setters. As I looked on down the valley to the next glade I could almost see a man with high leather boots laced to the knee. He was wearing a shooting coat and a round hat with a little 20-gauge L.C.Smith broken over his arm. As he turned a smile broke across a tanned, weathered face, and raising his handlebar mustache just enough to notice. I strained and blinked and he was gone.

Turning to whistle for Sally I found her standing at my side staring into the same glade that I had envisioned the old timer. Can dogs dream also? The old gunner may have been a fleeting daydream, but the cover and birds at hand were real and waiting.

The sun had dropped behind the high ridge and the cool, damp air was settling into the hollow, ideal conditions to scent feeding grouse. With the sense of urgency gone I rested the gun on my shoulder and walked slowly along inhaling the beauty of such a covert while Sally cut the valley into little sections. Her head was high and she reminded me of a mongoose searching the tall grass for a king cobra. Suddenly she seemed to hit an invisible pane of bullet proof glass, stacking up on point so hard she looked compressed like a black and white accordion. Jerking the gun from my shoulder I slid along side of her.

When nothing flushed I eased out to the side and then cut around in a half circle that took me to her front. There was a tangle of greenbrier around an old hawthorn with a few remaining haws. I stood still to see if the stillness would unnerve the bird. The only thing that happened was that it got quieter.

I told Sally what a great dog she was, thinking that my voice might put the grouse into flight. Like many of the day this one seemed glued to the ground. Nothing to do but put my head down and wade into the tangle and hope for the best. On the second step into the tangle I heard him start out. Only it wasn't him, it was them.

Two, three, four, five then silence. Still half bent over I had to back out of the tangle to see if I could at least see where they went when "here comes another" I caught myself saying out loud just as he cleared the tangle. The grouse could have gone any way but the way he did, but luck was with me and he banked to my left giving me a good shot at a skyline bird. After all these years I can still see him stretched out against the sky, tail fanned and neck outstretched. I mounted the gun while tracking him with my eyes. As soon as the gun hit my shoulder the picture looked right and I jerked the trigger. The grouse was only wing tipped and spiraled down. By the time he got his feet under him, Sally had him in her mouth. He was dead when she delivered him to my hand, another big, red phase Appalachian grouse. Three in the bag and the best hour still ahead.

In those early years it seemed important to take a limit of four birds if the opportunity presented itself. This would be the day! Sally was off again but all at once I realized our pristine glade had been swallowed up by older aged, mixed hardwoods. We had run our course, and with darkness seeping over the valley we turned and headed back. It was funny because, although we had just come this way, nothing looked the same as it did just an hour ago. I had a general idea of which direction to go and we headed out with Sally as fresh as any four year old I had ever hunted.

Sally was running to the side and front, like a smooth outrigger, when I heard a bird start to my left. It was nowhere near the dog or me and I couldn't understand why it had flushed. As I stood there I heard first another then two more. By now I had lost count of flushes, but I was sure the count had to be near thirty different birds. Those were the last birds we saw or heard that evening.

At dark we reached the first ridge top, and I could see the tiny flicker of light from the old lady's farmhouse a long way below. An easy, downhill walk back with Sally drooping, carrying her tail like a German Shepherd, she realized it was over for another day. All the way to the bottom I kept reliving the afternoon in my mind. I even wondered if Sally could recall her memories of this great day. The deer season would open on Monday and it would be three weeks before I could get back.

I hunted several days during the deer season but my heart wasn't in it. Twice during those weeks of waiting I shot up in my bed from a dead sleep to the thunder of grouse wings. Working, and hunting deer when I could, I spent many restless days and sleepless nights waiting for the time when Sally and I could walk over the ridge and into the *valley of the grouse*, as I now called it. It was new Year's Day before I found myself heading up the road towards Abbott. Since that time, I had mentioned my experience to Raymond Phillips of Buckhannon. Raymond was a native of the county and as my story unraveled he listened with great interest. Finally he said that many years ago, when he was a boy, he had heard the old timers talk of an entire settlement back in the very hills I had described. He went on to say for some reason all had left or died and the settlement was abandoned completely. He couldn't quite remember the name but was sure he knew that was the place.

It was cold and there was about an inch of snow on the ground as I neared the old lady's house. The first thing I noticed was the big, orange signs. POSTED-NO HUNTING OR TRESPASSING. When I pulled into the yard I saw two men carrying out furniture to a pickup. I introduced myself and asked about the lady who lived there. I was informed that she had died. She had told her pastor that she had no further will to live and that she was ready to die. The man I was talking to finally told me he was her pastor and that she had left the property to the church. He asked my business and I explained I was a friend of the people who had lived there and they said I could hunt. He quickly pointed out the no hunting signs and informed me that the church would sell the property in the spring.

We talked for a while and I guess he finally felt sorry for me. Anyway, he said that since I had driven 60 miles I could hunt this one last time. I thanked him and slipped the bell around Sally's neck. We wasted little time in the hollow on this side of the ridge; we knew where we wanted to go and headed for it. Soon the little patch ended but the clearing didn't look the same. Was it the snow or had we made a little wrong turn? It made no real difference as I knew we had to cross the high ridge at the top of the hollow and head to the left and then drop into our grouse heaven. Again I felt this sense of urgency sweeping over me. Again I was marching ahead as a man possessed. I had to get into the hollow and find the birds we had left there.

Topping the ridge I could not see the tops of the pines that led me to the old foundation the first time. Had I gone too far to the right or had I not gone far enough? These questions were echoing through my head as Sally worked in front of me slowly, deliberately, without her usual flash and drive. She too seemed unsure of her surroundings. None of what we saw looked like grouse cover. The trees were all too big, too old and with no ground cover. I decided we would just drop into the valley ahead and then hunt back and forth until we cut the valley we were looking for.

Well, we did drop down and hunt back and forth. We also hunted to the front and to the back. We crossed several little ridges on either side. In all we hunted for almost two hours without finding our Tinkhamtown, our Valhalla, our grouse hunters' dream covert. Not only did we not find it but we never flushed a single grouse.

I was dejected as I started back to the top of the ridge. Sally had quit hunting as she recognized there was really no grouse cover to hunt. As I neared the top I started to remember how great it had been that day when we first entered our lost valley. The farther I went, and the more memories of Sally standing on point as two, three and four grouse roared out from under nose, the higher my spirits soared. By the time we started down the other side I was stepping pretty lively and thinking of the afternoon's hunt still to come. I had walked through bird hunter's heaven, and the Good Lord smiled heavily on me. The Good Lord smiles on some of us more than we deserve, and twenty years later I would again walk the Road To Tinkhamtown.

Tinkhamtown Revisited

This time Jan Riffe would be with me and can attest to the truth of what follows. By now our good friend, and mentor, George Burroughs had introduced us to the great grouse hunting of the Lake States. We knew the country well enough now and he would cut us loose on our own to explore and find new coverts. While getting gas at a small crossroad station, on the border of Michigan and Wisconsin, we mentioned to an old-timer that we were grouse hunting. He allowed as how if a man went to a certain road, parked and headed due west he might find a lot of "pats." That's all it took. We have chased the wild goose all over the range of the upland bird, and our emotions began to soar.

Jan asked what I thought of the old man. He felt were we off again with goose feathers in our eyes instead of grouse feathers. I told him I didn't think so. There was a twinkle in the old man's eyes. I could sense excitement in his voice as he talked about it. He had that Rip Van Winkle air about him, that magical quality that draws the innocent, the trusting. Maybe I just wanted it to be true. In any event, searching for a new covert choked with grouse has its own excitement and becomes a part of so many hunts that I can't venture to count the times of success and failure. We had enjoyed a good week, and to find a great new covert on the last day of the hunt would give us something to look forward to the rest of the year.

The old timer told us that, as a boy, he had worked in a logging camp as an assistant cook. The "pats" were so thick, and he cooked so many, the loggers got tired of them. He said there was a network of old roads that interlaced through the old openings that once had been the camp and loading area. He had been back there five years ago, guiding for a "sport" from Flint, and they had seen pats all along the little grown up roads.

According to the old man, the sport had shot several as he walked the roads that were covered with clover and the tiny mushrooms that grow in that country. That checked out, as we had long ago learned the importance of the greens in a grouse's diet. During our first visits to the Lake States, George Burroughs had instructed us to look for salad. To find grouse in this country, he would say, look for the salad: a variety of tiny green plants like clover, strawberry leaves, wintergreen and the like. Throw in the little mushrooms and you have a grouse's gourmet dinner plate.

The old man had pointed to the west with the stump of a forefinger lost to a sawmill accident many years ago. We asked if we could take him home, but he just smiled and said that there was no road into his cabin. I was still taking to him when he just turned his back to me and walked across the road and disappeared into the thick brush. Jan and I looked at each other, and without a word got into the truck. "What do you think," Jan asked? "Lets go," I answered and we were off down the dirt road with a plume of dust hanging in the air behind us.

Not to miss the directions, I had written down every word he said. The road made the two 90 degree bends and on the left was the gravel pit. Another mile or so and we came to the sandy banks of the deep-running tea colored creek. We hesitated as we studied the rough sawed planks of the bridge. It showed recent traffic, and appeared to be sturdy enough. We crossed it quickly, as if we might escape harm should it collapse beneath us.

When we came to a rotting sawdust pile the size of a large house, we were at the designated spot. From here he told us to walk downhill until we found the trace of an old grown up road leading off to the west. "It will go down and disappear into the big woods. When it ends, bear to the north west until you cross the little swamp. When you come out of the swamp you will be into the covert you are looking for. Once in, simply walk the trails and let the dogs hunt the edges. You will find all the pats you want."

"This is the place," I told Jan.

"Or one just like it," he said as I drove the truck into the thicket to get off the remains of an old road. It sure didn't look like grouse country from what we could see. It looked old and dead, the ground was black with none of the green we had hoped for. But the old man's description was too vivid to give up here. Pepper, my young English setter, hit the ground and started to search for the *drummer*. Jan would hunt his setter Patch.

Jan and I decided to head to the end of the lane, as the old man suggested, and waste no time looking for anything else. Pepper was popping in and out of the lane in an attempt to stay ahead of us as we walked along at a hurried pace. Patch was staying pretty close to Jan as this was the young dog's first year in the grouse woods. It was early afternoon but we figured we had a ways to go.

Everything was as the old man described, the big timber, the downhill slope and then the little swamp lined with tag alder. As we climbed a small bank we popped up on to what appeared to be a large expanse of rolling country. Surely this was the spot but where were the roads he talked of, where was the salad? Regardless, it was grouse country. We spread out a little and Pepper crossed in front, to our left, and disappeared into one of the many, tiny swells that seemed to dot the country. As we walked toward the little depression we realized her bell was silent.

The pace quickened as we headed for where we had last seen her. I got to the rim of the swale first. There, in the middle of the depression, stood the snow-white little setter. Guess what? She was on a soft, dark green carpet, ankle deep in clover and strawberry leaves, standing in a ghost of an old road. We were there!

I motioned to Jan to circle as I went directly to the dog. He was in position now and I started to close the distance. Jan was screened by low, thick aspen but I could see blotches of orange. Pepper was locked in on an old stump that stood in the middle of some head high aspen whips. Jan signaled a "whoa" to Patch to prevent an accidental flush. I reached out with my left hand, holding the 28 gauge double in the other, and parted the dog hair aspen. I took one more step and the grouse exploded out of the forest floor. I was bent a little and I remember seeing a swirl of leaves, not 20 feet in front of me, where he sprang into the air.

I had no chance for a shot as he hooked back to the right towards Jan. "Here he..." Boom! barked Jan's 16 gauge Winchester 21 before I could say "...comes." Pepper rushed forward and I could hear her hesitate when she got to the downed bird. In a flash she was back at my side with a beautiful gray phase grouse draped out of her mouth.

I knelt to take the grouse from her soft mouth. I was still kneeling, showing young Patch the grouse, when Jan walked over to see his first bird of the day. "See what you are kneeling in?" he asked. Looking down I expected to see a pile of dog, bear or deer droppings. Instead there they were, the tiny mushrooms surrounded by clover. Jan carefully tucked the grouse in his game bag, and we were off.

It was 3:00 P.M. and entering into that enchanted part of the grouse hunter's afternoon. I have found that, on most days, I can move as many grouse in the last two or three hours of daylight as I can in the rest of the day. The grouse will come out to feed during this period and the scent seems to hang in the cool, damp evening air. Most of the best dog work will come as the fingers of long, cool shadows pierce the afternoon grouse coverts. We walked another fifty yards on the old road and came to a fork where the forest had overtaken the log loading area from the old man's era.

I would hunt to the east and Jan would go on to the west. We would meet at the truck at dark. The wind off Lake Superior had died now and the covert became extremely quiet. As Jan and I moved away from each other Patches' bell was as clear and sharp as if his dog were with me. Pepper squirted out in the road about 50 yards ahead, saw me and dove back in where the road made a sharp bend to the left. I was tracking her by the little sleigh bell as she worked the cover along the edge. I am always amazed by how abruptly the bell stops when she hits a point. This time was no different. There was no tinkle, ending in silence, as the bell's clapper made its last swing. Instead it was if some invisible force had plucked Pepper from the covert, bell and all, dead silence in front of me. Only the clear jingle of Patch's bell sounded in the distance as he and Jan hunted their country.

I hurried ahead to the bend in the road where Pepper had been swallowed up by the black Michigan earth. Looking ahead it appeared as if I was following a soft, green path flecked with red and brown where the strawberry leaves and mushrooms were sprinkled among the clover. The road snaked through grays, browns, and dark greens. I was in a tunnel lined with aspen, tag alder and birch, with a green, tweed carpet that disappeared at each bend. No sign of the bell.

In a few yards I saw splotches of white and then the whole dog. Pepper was about 20 yards into a little corner where some tag alder and aspen came together to bound the road of salad. She was looking out toward the road,

Tinker backs Tomba, who pins a grouse in the open, feeding under a hawthorn. Even in the open it is a long way to the game bag.

and I knew she had the bird pinned between her and the road. No doubt he had been feeding on the salad and moved to the edge when he heard her coming.

I moved up the road towards her with the 28 gauge Bill Hanas double in the ready position. Another few steps and I would be in good shooting range. I was thinking 'If I can just get to that small, twisted aspen,' when the grouse went out. A flash of movement was all I saw as the bird streaked away low back into the covert behind Pepper. She turned her head but never moved and I realized there may be another. I took another step and heard a grouse start out, then another. I saw them both at the same time.

One was crossing the road, and the other was going directly away as I swung and mounted. Here is where the speed of a light, well balanced gun shines. The gun hit my shoulder as the barrels covered the crossing bird. In the same instant I jerked the trigger and 3/4 ounces of 9's shredded the remaining leaves on a small tag alder. The bird was hit but not hard. I kept swinging and hit him hard with the left barrel, sending him spinning to the ground. At that same instant another grouse thundered out of the cover at the right edge of the road and came back high over my head.

All I could do was point an empty gun at him and say "bang." I turned to see Pepper coming with a wing over one eye. She seemed to be prancing, unsure of where her foot was going to touch down. I was taking the bird out of her mouth when I heard Jan's 16 boom off in the distance. I remember thinking he was getting pretty far from the truck.

The road seemed to circle now and checking the compass I found that I was headed directly away from the truck. Another 75 yards and I came to another fork. I was standing there deciding which to take when a grouse thundered out behind me. I whirled around just in time to seem him cross the road behind me and disappear into the shadows. I had walked within ten yards of the bird and he had held.

Again, "boom, boom," off in Jan's direction. Two such quick shots meant a clean miss or a double. "Boom, boom" again. What in the world is he into, I thought, as Pepper and I started down the left fork.

Fifty yards and I heard a bird off to the left but didn't see him. Pepper heard him too and stopped. In a second she started in the direction where we heard him. Suddenly, that abrupt silence. "Must be pointing where the bird just went out," I was thinking as I stopped. "In a moment she will realize the scent is dissipating and she will be moving." The seconds turned into a minute and still no movement. I gave a soft whistle but still nothing. Then it dawned on fast old Frank that she was pointing another bird.

It was thicker here and I had to worm my way back into the cover. Bending low I could see her stretched out in a crouched, intense point. She looked as if she were ready to pounce. I pushed forward and a branch reached out and snagged my hat off my head. Why would anyone stop to pick up a hat when the dog was on point not 30 yards ahead? I have no idea, but I did. I was bent over, had the hat in my hand, trying to push on backward through the tangle, when the bird went out. Only it wasn't a bird, it was a pair of birds, and straight away, as if in slow motion, they went.

There went my chance for a true double I was thinking when again, "boom, boom," came from off in the distance. Must be into a flight of woodcock, I was telling myself when Pepper made a little circle out toward Jan's shot. She was coming back to the road when she slammed into a point not 20 yards from me. I took one step toward her and out he roared. The trees were taller here and the grouse was going high. I was tracking him when he swung out across the opening the road presented in the sky. The barrels passed his nose and I hit the trigger. For a moment he hung there, suspended against a blue sky streaked with long golden shadows of sunlight.

He was dead in the air, no flapping or turning or cartwheels. Instead it was as if I had tossed a dead grouse into the sky. At 20 yards he had been centered by the load of hard 9's. I see no appreciable difference in the 20 and the 28. When I am on them with either I kill them just as dead. When I am not on them I miss just as shamefully.

I shot one more and missed two as I worked back towards the truck. All the while I was tracking Jan by his shots across the thicket. The roads seemed to be a maze and I was almost sure I was walking in circles. I realized I was hurrying as if to get to the next grouse before I dealt with the one at hand. I seemed driven to find the next and the next. They were everywhere! And the cover was as ideal as any I had ever hunted in the Lake States. The right age aspen and the right mixture of aspen, alder, and witchhazel. And then there was the salad; everywhere the forest clearings and the road was choked with the salad.

I would shoot and then Jan would shoot. Finally I could hear Patch's bell and Jan's voice as he talked to his dog. I rounded a little bend and there they were coming at us on the same road. "Well, how many did you flush," was his greeting?

I explained that I had lost count at 15 or 16. He said he had stopped counting at 20. Neither one of us had taken a limit but it made no difference. We were caught up in the magic of this cover.

"Birds are everywhere," Jan continued. He went on to explain that all he was doing was following the maze of roads. His young dog had pointed some, and flushed some. He said that he didn't know why but after the first few he seemed to be rushing from one bird to the next, from one patch of cover along the road to the next as if to flush that bird and go to the next. He had experienced the same sense of urgency that engulfed Pepper and me. As we looked around to get our bearings we realized we were in the middle of the remains of the old logging camp. The forest had reclaimed the clearing but there were foundation stones, pieces of old equipment and skeletons of old logs scattered about in the bracken fern.

We checked the compass and found that again we were headed away from the truck. It was 4:30 now and we had at least an hour's walk. Taking a reading we decided to follow the road that went in the direction of the truck. The action continued. We couldn't go 100 yards without flushing a bird. Some were on the ground and a few were already in the trees for the night. Singles, pairs and triples, they rocketed away from the road at our approach. The dogs were frantic. Patch was worn out but Pepper was caught up in the excitement. I brought Pepper in to my side while we sized up the situation.

We decided that with darkness approaching so rapidly we needed to get out and not try to kill another grouse. There was no need to kill another. We each had birds, the dogs had excellent work and we had again found The Road Into Tinkhamtown. This is where we would start the season next fall.

The road we were following veered away from the direction we needed to go. We left the road and plunged into the brush. Nothing looked the same. The forest was different, there was more water, and we seemed to be going downhill instead of up as we thought we should. There appeared to be more hardwoods instead of aspen and all of it was too big. Still, we had learned long ago that, unless you are in the Bermuda Triangle, you should trust you compass.

The first stars were out now and we could see what appeared to be a break in the forest up ahead. Soon we were standing at the edge of an old grown up pasture field. We had parked on the edge of a pasture but it had cattle in it. Staying on the line of the compass we began to cross the old field. As we topped the crest we could see the glint of metal in the distance. Sure enough, another five minutes walking brought us to the truck.

Dogs loaded, we sat in the truck for a moment enjoying a warm shot of coffee. Looking back over the area we had just come from, it now appeared as if we had been in the center of a very large bowl that was rimmed on all sides by little ridges. It seemed there was no way to go in or come out where we did without crossing a very large ridge. Surely we would have noticed such a steep climb. Was there a low gap in the ridge, a road that took us through the ridge instead of up over it? We would decide that next year at our return; for now it made no difference. Jan marked the spot where we were parked on our map, drew a little road straight ahead and penciled in "The Road To Tinkhamtown." Beside it he wrote: "A maze of roads covered with salad. At least 50 flushes. Six grouse shot. Start the next season here!!" And we did.

As you get older you notice that you no sooner clean your gun and cut the grass a few times, and it is time to go again. For the bird hunter, life becomes a blur, a speeding train increasing its momentum as it heads down the tracks, through a tunnel of aspen, greenbrier, grapevines and hawthorn, steamrolling towards one's own mortality. Depressing thought, but the point is, do as my loving old friend George Burroughs does. Live every moment to its fullest and never look back except to see if your dog is coming.

Plans were made, the day arrived, and Jan and I were again heading up that long, straight highway into the Lake States. Sleep came hard our first night as visions of covey after covey of grouse, rising out of the salad on the old roads, kept me squirming in my bed. Jan was up first and announced it appeared to be a beautiful day. Lunches packed, dogs loaded, maps reviewed, there was no question where we were headed. Down the road to Tinkhamtown we went.

We passed the little store where we had met the old logger and I wondered if he was still alive. Soon we got to our first turn off where we had crossed the bridge over the deep, dark river. Problem was, no bridge. Back to the little store we went for help and, hopefully, directions. The same cheerful, little old lady was behind the counter. I described the old logger with the stub of a finger and asked if he was about anywhere. She lowered her head a little and said that he had passed away on Christmas Day.

She had no idea where we were trying to go and sent us down the road to the next gas station. The young man there knew the bridge and said that since it really didn't go to anything, the county wasn't going to replace it after the washout that past spring. We showed him on our map where we wanted to go, careful to keep a finger over the writing we had penciled in. He said he felt sure we could make a circle of about eight miles and come into the same area from another direction. The road he pointed out appeared to go where we wanted to go, so off we went.

After some compass readings and downright guessing we came to what we felt was the spot. Ahead rose what appeared to be the kind of high ridge we had seen from the other side. Nothing to do but take a reading and plunge in. There wasn't much conversation as we readied the dogs, stuffed a few extra shells into our vests and started into the cover. The first part looked good as we remembered, big timber and a little standing water. We came to the end of this type cover but there were no little roads, just more smaller timber and grass. The forest floor was covered with a thick, heavy grass, the kind that grouse and woodcock avoid. One thing we knew for sure, there was no grass in our Tinkhamtown.

The day was young and we decided the best way to find the covert was to separate. When one of us found the covert the other would know by the shooting and come running. Silence never seemed so deafening as it did that morning. The longer the morning went the more the silence hurt my ears. The cover was not right. There was too much water, too much grass, and the forest was too old. I kept searching in every direction for something that looked familiar. Pepper was covering the ground well but never once did she even appear to hit scent, even old scent. I went up hill, down hill to the east and west, all the while listening for Jan to shoot. It never happened.

After three hours of wandering through this old growth forest I came to a relic of a road. Instead of salad it was covered with rocks and pine needles Surely it would lead into the covert we sought. Pepper was hunting both sides as I tried to recognize something from the year past. After 30 minutes we rounded a bend and came face to face with Patch and Jan. Both of them had dejected looks on their faces.

Sitting on a giant old stump we compared notes. Not a grouse flushed and not a sign of the country we searched for. Twice more, during that ten day trip, we tried to find our Tinkhamtown only to be beaten by the old growth forest. We found other coverts that year and hunted some of our old ones. We found enough birds to satisfy the needs of our dogs but that particular covert haunted us daily.

Oh yes, we returned the following year also. Not only was the little bridge still out but most of the road going to it had also washed out. We resigned ourselves to the fact that the Road to Tinkhamtown was gone forever. And maybe it should be. After all, the good Lord had let old Frank walk that road twice in his lifetime. That is two times more than most people I have talked to ever get to walk it. The rest had no idea what I was talking about. Yes, there is a Tinkhamtown. It is in the aspen of the Lake States, and in the briery tangles of Appalachia. It's in the damp little rills of New England and the brush choked creek bottoms of Montana. It is in the fantasies of a few bird hunters. And if you are lucky and hunt long and hard enough, you too will find yourself walking The Road To Tinkhamtown.

Mysteries of the Mountains

If you wander through the mountains long enough and far enough things that can't be explained will occur.

Intruders on Hallowed Ground

There's a vast plateau between Rowelsburg, Kingwood and Tunnelton, West Virginia. The east side drops off sharply to the mighty Cheat River. Tom Stalnaker introduced me to this area after he found it while turkey hunting. If you could see it from the air it resembles an octopus. A large round center with several drooping, outreaching arms or hollows. An extensive strip mining operation went through the area in the 50's and 60's. The only reclamation during that period was to plant autumn olive bushes to help hold the loose soil. While the agriculture department has classified the autumn olive as a noxious weed, it is one of the most beneficial of all plants for the grouse of Appalachia. This high plateau is a tangle of autumn olive, multiflora rose, greenbrier and grape vines, a grouse hunter's paradise. If you wanted to show someone what classic grouse cover was supposed to look like, this is where you would take them.

It was late October when I pulled out into a little clearing just over the west lip of the mountain. Jack Frost had already danced across this country dripping color and setting the mountain top ablaze as he went. Tomba and

Pixie were scratching at the door to their box realizing that we were at the spot for the day's hunt. There are two old jeep roads into this country and both are straight up. There are no houses for miles, and one old fence at the very edge of the plateau.

Here a gunner and his dogs can roam with not a sign of a building, poster, or hard road. This is Appalachian Grouse country. Like much of the country in the Mountain State, this belongs to the coal company that stripped the land. They cut the timber, take the coal, replant some, and the land sits there in agony healing its wounds. This disrupting of the surface is what creates the new growth that our grouse need to survive and prosper. While we curse the appearance of the open wounds that are left, we must realize that it creates grouse habitat.

I decided to hunt the dogs separately, as it was to be an all day affair and I wanted a fresh dog for the afternoon hunt. With his orange collar and bell on Tomba was prancing at my feet while I stuffed a few 20 gauge 8's into my pocket and dropped two into the old Belgian Browning I was carrying. On the last day of the previous season I had flushed three different woodcock. I felt sure this would be a day of both grouse and woodcock.

The sky was a blue that only The Big Man can paint. In it he had dabbed small, round, puffy, white clouds. There was just enough breeze to keep them moving from west to east. "This would be a good day", I told Tomba as I cast him into the covert. The grapes were on the ground so we decided to follow the ridge as it weaved in and out of the grape vines that laced the hardwoods.

It was easy going with an old trail leading into the country where we were headed. I was taking my time and letting Tomba work first one side of the trail and then the other. He plunged into a tangle at the bend up ahead and then silence. I stopped for a just a second to size up the approach of his point. After four or five steps I saw him stretched out on the left side of the trail, fixed on a tangle of vines around an old fallen tree. The woods to the left was fairly open so this is where I decided to try and flush the bird. Making a quick half circle to the right I was now coming at the dog from his right. He didn't turn his head, indicating that he knew he had his bird locked on solidly. Just a few more steps and I would be in good shooting range. Beside the dog now and still no flush. A soft whoa as I passed the dog and another step and a pause. The pause is all it took.

I could hear him beating the tangle with his wings well before he broke into sight. When he did, he didn't go down through the open woods as I thought he would. Instead, he bored right up to the tree tops and then started to level off. The charge of 8's caught him just as he reached the top of his flight. He tumbled down through the tree tops in a shower of multi colored leaves.

Tomba followed his flight at the shot and scooped him up without missing a step. He made a little circle and then stopped with the bird in his mouth. He just stood there as I said fetch, dead bird. Then I could see the problem. The bird had one wing completely over Tomba's eyes. I told him to stay and walked over to him. We took a moment to admire the big cock bird with the reddish brown color phase the Appalachians are famous for, and carefully tucked him into the game bag so as not to ruffle those feathers.

Oh, if only I could release him again to fly another day! But I can't, and this killing of the bird is part of the hunt. We took him fair and square, on his terms and now we were off to look for another. Tomba was working his cover with grace and ease. I stopped for a moment to get my bearings and realized the trail had disappeared and we had been swallowed up by the mountain. A quick check of the compass showed the direction where we planned to go. I had not been in this section of the mountain before, and there were no old roads or trails, just solid cover. We were headed up now and the terrain was steeper than it had appeared from where we started.

The cover was looking better with every step. Tomba was searching every likely-looking clump of brush. He looked like a black and white metronome arm, swinging back from left to right, when a grouse catapulted from a grape tangle and bore away, high through the trees. The leaves were getting a little noisy now as the heat of mid day began to dry them some. Tomba didn't hear the bird and I decided to see what he would do when he hit the spot from where it flew. In a few seconds he was nearing the spot but just before he got to where I thought he should strike the scent, he froze.

The wind was wrong and I didn't think he could smell the bird that had just flown out. I started to him and as I reached good shooting distance he softened a little. "Must have been where the bird walked," I thought, as I continued to him. I have hunted with these dogs long enough to know that they don't just point to be pointing. They smell something that triggers that pointing instinct and I trust them enough to walk in and see. I know that if the bird leaves, the dog will break and continue searching. Only, this time, Tomba didn't break. He just stood there, dropping his tail and lowering his head, looking more like a farm collie than a class setter. "Maybe a snake or a turtle," I thought, as I neared him.

He was looking around now and I became aware that the sun had dropped behind some fast moving clouds and the woods became darker. When I got nearly beside the dog I saw something shiny and gray in front of him. He

Nestled on top of a rugged Preston County, WV mountain, the author came across three neatly laid tombstones dating to 1854. There was no apparent beginning or end to the old road where they were buried, just one of the many mysteries we run across in the mountains of Appalachia.

was nearly standing on it, smelling it and looking back up at me. Then, through the forest litter I saw them. I brushed the debris away with my hand and stood transfixed, staring down at a line of three neatly laid tombstones!

A cold shiver went over me for no good reason. I had been sweating some while climbing up the ridge and I guess the dark wind that blew through this tunnel under the trees had pierced my damp shirt. There was no other good reason. Tomba just stood there sniffing one and then the other. I couldn't help but wonder why, with no sign of a mountain farm or settlement for several miles, they were buried up here. "James W. Riley 1854-1920." I stepped back a few feet when the realization hit me.

One hundred and forty years ago this man had entered these mountains. Were the others sons, what had happened to them, where did they live, why were they buried up here so high on the mountain with no sign of any family plot? I wonder if they were grouse hunters? This was the kind of place a grouse hunter would want to be laid to rest with his sons who hunted with him. When I began to look around I found that we were under a complete canopy of trees. For all practical purposes it resembled one of those big funeral canopies they put up over a grave.

That wasn't the surprising point, though. We were also on a little piece of old forest road. It didn't appear to go anywhere or come from anywhere but it was a section of road approximately 50 yards long. It began in a thicket and ended in a thicket with no other indication of a road that I could pick up. If the tombstones were laid at their feet we were standing on the graves. Tomba and I backed off and started back the way we had come.

Tomba didn't resume his hunting, he just walked at heel with a low head and tail uncharacteristic of him. When we were about 200 yards from the spot of the tombstones the clouds opened, and the bright October sun again lighted up the forest. As if on key Tomba raced ahead and into the covert again. I stopped and looked back up the mountain. Did that grouse live near the tombstones, I wondered? Was the grouse the soul of the old man, free for eternity, to roam these mountains that mean so much to us mountaineers who live here?

"Forgive these two intruders, old friends, we didn't realize we were standing on hallowed ground," I said, as I continued to follow Tomba around the mountain. I went back three times that winter and tried to find the same old piece of road that led up to the tombstone covert, but I can't find it again. Search as I have, it eludes me. Was it a figment of a tired hunter's imagination? Is it really up there? I know the answer as I sit here looking at the slides of the tombstones, so clear and sharp. Maybe that is just the way it is supposed to be. Maybe some places are not meant to be disturbed. Maybe that grouse can't be hit or killed anyway!

CHAPTER 2

FANTAILS AND SHARPTAILS

A Grouse Is A Grouse, Is A Grouse

It had been six years but with a little backtracking and searching we could now see the plowed field, just as we remembered it. Bordered by aspen, spruce, and low shrubs, it is one of the most picturesque pieces of bird cover a gunner with pointing dogs could ever hope to walk through.

There wasn't much conversation, and you could chew on the tension that hung heavy in the air as we turned off the gravel road and into the edge of the flax stubble. In 1987 the greatest concentration of ruffed grouse this half century had seen covered this very country spread out in front of us. In 1988 it started to crash and in '92 and '93 you were hard pressed to locate a pair of ruffs in a hard day of hunting. The sharptail grouse were there, but not many of the ruffs.

In 1987 we had afternoons of 40 to 50 grouse moved, not flushes but separate grouse flown! It's hard to believe, but others, like biologist Don Rousch, were there and can testify. For those not accustomed to hunting grouse at the extreme northern edge of their range, it is hard to picture this phenomenon, but in this far north country the birds both explode and crash at extremes. This is backed by biological studies carried out by Rousch, who has been involved in the study of grouse with Canadian biologists for over 25 years. It is hard to imagine, but some natives, like Rick Swenty, tell us that there was an even higher cycle in 1977!

All this was running through our minds as we turned off into the stubble. Our contacts told us that this was the turnaround year, that broods of both sharptails and ruffs were being seen. Sliding to a stop in the loose dirt, we were surprised and a little stunned, but excited, when a flock of about a dozen sharptail grouse got up in front of the truck bumper. We watched as they cleared the plowed field and fanned out into the clumps of young aspen. What a sight! The shimmering, golden leaves of the aspen contrasted with the dark green spruce trees scattered about. All were aglow in the late afternoon sun as the white and gray wings disappeared into the low cover.

It was getting late and we just wanted to locate the area for tomorrow's hunt, and exercise the dogs after the long drive from the Twin Cities. Jan would take his dog to the right edge of the cover, and I would head Pixie and Tomba off to the left. The dogs were anxious and were cutting the field as they slashed back and forth. I was glad it was 300 yards to the cover. The distance would take a little of their edge off rather than throwing them in right on top of the birds, if there were any there. We were working deeper into the cover now, and I was just standing, enjoying the beauty of well-breed pointers and setters as they flowed over the ground.

Tomba was cutting across from the left with the sun at his back. I watched him go behind a small clump of 15-foot high aspen. I saw Pixie coming from the right, by a little gnarled spruce, when I realized that Tomba was still behind the little clump of aspen. About the time that Fast Frank realized he had a dog on point, Pixie snapped into an intense back. They were frozen in time on this carpet of golds, greens, and tans that only Mother Nature can lay before man and dog. They had a nice piece of bird work here, and I wanted to kill the bird for them. I remember thinking, "I have you now, Mr. Sharptail," as I squirmed into the clump of short aspen.

I eased into the aspens and had to duck under a branch to get through. When I did, a "staub," (that's Appalachian slang for a broken limb protruding from a tree) caught the opening of my game bag. There I stood, hooked in a bent position, with two magnificent pointing dogs glued to the ground in front of me. Only one thing to do; lunge forward and break free. I came off that tree like a 200-pound ballerina turned fullback! But the dogs never moved and nothing flushed. As I took the next step, the leaves erupted in a flurry of wings. To my amazement, the wings weren't white, they were brown, and the tail wasn't sharp, it was fanned!

A ruffed grouse in low open cover that comes out under your feet is a rather easy target. At the crack of the 20 gauge O/U, the bird stopped in a puff of brown feathers. Dead in the air from the one ounce load of 71/2s', the bird fluttered little before Tomba returned with his first Manitoba ruffed grouse. I sat with the dogs for a moment on the warm carpet of grasses to admire a beautiful grouse similar to the color phase I'm familiar with. In Manitoba, the ruffs run mostly to the gray phase but several of the reddish-brown ones show up also.

Jan Riffe and Tinker show that, in western Canada, the range of the ruffed grouse and the sharptailed grouse overlap, offering some of the best combination gunning in the uplands.

The sun was down as I started back to the truck. I had heard Jan shoot twice and figured he had gotten into the sharptails we saw sail into the cover. Back at the truck, Jan related that he had indeed found the sharptails, and in addition he also flew a fantailed ruffed grouse. Thirty minutes of hunting, and we had two ruffs and a sharptail all shot over solid points!

That evening, the third member of our party arrived from Flint, Michigan. George Burroughs, at 80-plus years, is the most devoted and enthusiastic bird hunter I know. He had driven for three days, alone except for the three Elhew pointers who have the run of his Land Rover, to meet us in central Manitoba. George had been there with Jan and I in 1987, and like us was waiting for the day he could return.

The next day we decided to sample other areas to see if indeed the cycle was turning around. We were driving along one of the endless gravel roads that bordered a stubble field. The grain had been recently harvested, but like always there was a lot left in the field. Going slow to size up the cover along the field, again we almost ran into a flock of sharptails. They sailed across the stubble to fan out into some scattered, bigger aspen. There was more grass here than where we had seen them the day before. Checking our plat map, we knew this was Crown Land and open to hunting. We decided to follow them as they had gone into some cover we planned to hunt anyway.

We would hunt together this time with one dog. We let Pixie out, and across the field we went. Just as she cleared the stubble, we saw her throw her head into the air and take a few stiff-legged, cat-like steps. Then she froze with a nose full of sharptail scent. I motioned for Jan, but he had already seen her. He moved in and would shoot any birds that came out of the right while I would cover the left. We moved up even with the dog, but nothing happened. I told him to get ready as I moved in farther, but still nothing. I was just about to tell him they had run off in front of her point when one got up not five feet from me and the dog. It made the mistake of circling back to the right and in front of Jan.

When his 16-gauge Winchester 21 cracked, I saw the bird cartwheel. At the report of his gun, a bird got up on my side, and at the same time I noticed Pixie still standing there. It broke out to the left across a bare, plowed field where it met a load of 71/2s'. I broke the gun to load and another bird got up, then another and then two more. But we had a pair down and let Pixie retrieve them before we went on.

Finding a covey of sharptails in each piece of cover that looked good confirmed what we had hoped for; the grouse were back! Pixie was prancing around anxious to go after the other birds she knew were sprinkled around in the cover ahead of her. I released her and she headed into a little clump of aspen mixed with willow. Ten yards from the edge she put on the brakes and stacked up into a hard point. She stopped so suddenly that she looked six inches shorter. Jan saw her at the same time I did and started moving in her direction. I stood still as he entered the thin stand of timber, grass and willow. "Clack, clack clack, clack, clack" and the air was filled with brown and gray missiles. They came spinning out in all directions. I heard Jan shoot twice as I mounted my gun, tacking an in-comer. It was a high house eight, only the bird was bigger and slower. As the barrels covered the bird, I jerked the trigger. Hit head on, with a full charge of 7 1/2's, the bird was graveyard dead when it fell at my feet. We had taken enough sharptails from this covey and decided to spend the remaining daylight looking for ruffed grouse.

Late afternoon found us going back into familiar country that bordered a big, dry lake bed. This cover is identical to what you find in the Lake States. It is made up of aspen, spruce, natural clearings with wintergreen berries, and a very thick understory of witch hazel brush. It surrounds little hay meadow valleys that wind back, serpentine fashion, into spruce, willow and aspen cover. These little clearings and hay meadows draw the sharptails and thicker cover attracts the ruffed grouse. It is here that the ranges of the two overlap to form some of the finest upland gunning over pointing dogs that North America has to offer.

At first you will think that some of these immense aspen barrens are too thin to hold ruffed grouse. You will think that the edges are too thick for sharptails. What you have to remember is that this is all native, undisturbed cover and grass where these birds have lived since time began. Ruffed grouse and sharptails both where here before man and his plow. The clearings and the plow just enhanced the cover, which helped the birds to flourish.

The rest of the week went about the same. Some days we had more flushes, and some we had fewer. The obvious fact was that the birds are coming back! Talking to a local hunter, the only one we have found in years of hunting up there who has pointing dogs, and who gets off the road in search of grouse, our thoughts were confirmed. He hunts a lot, raises and sells setters, and knows his country and his birds. He agreed that the birds were coming back and that the prediction of another high in the late 1990's should be right on schedule.

We left Rick and headed into hills. The first year we came to Manitoba we spent the better part of a day searching for *the hills*. During that time we met Ben, a farmer who came to Manitoba from Eastern Europe as a child. Like most of the natives of Manitoba, Ben was as friendly and helpful as if we had know him for years. He took us into his modest home where his wife insisted that we stay for lunch. These are hard working people who live in a harsh, desolate land. We saw pictures of their children, and they told us that there were no young people here anymore. As soon as they got old enough they headed for Winnipeg or the other bigger cities in Canada. The children had grown up watching their parents work day and night to plant and harvest, and most wanted nothing to do with it. They didn't have the bond with the earth that their parents brought with them when they came from Europe.

We enjoyed our visit with Ben, and the bologna sandwich, cheese and hot tea that his wife fixed us for lunch was an added treat. But our clock was running and we had impatient dogs in the truck. We explained to Ben that we were after the ruffed grouse. Like others we had talked to, he sent us into the hills where he often saw them as he traveled the gravel roads to and from his fields.

He showed us on the map where the hills were and we were off with a stream of dust trailing behind the truck. Even though this country is referred to as the pothole country of Canada it can be extremely dry during September and October. Because of this you always need to carry enough water for the dogs. We watched carefully for the hills in the distance, and thought we had gone far enough to be right in the middle of them. We drove and drove but no hills could we find. Finally, after making three trips through the area, we thought we had marked as the hills, we decided that it was getting late, and that if we were going to hunt this afternoon we had better pick a spot and hunt. We would check with Ben again tomorrow and find the hills where the ruffs were.

We picked an area where a large, circular field flowed back into some sparse clumps of aspen mixed in with gnarly, twisted, dwarf, spruce trees. Jan decided to go off to the right and I to the left, meeting at the back end to compare notes. We were skirting the field and getting farther and farther away from each other when I heard the crack of Jan's gun. Looking in his direction I saw a half dozen sharptails glide across the field and into the cover behind us. Ginny cut across in front of me and plunged into the bush on my left. I caught flashes of her as she hit the openings. She whirled with her head into the wind and went on point with her left rear leg off the ground. I started for her and made a mental note to pick a single out of the covey when the sharptails went into the air.

I was by her side now and still no whir of wings. This must be a covey of young sharptails, I was thinking, as I gingerly stepped past the frozen dog. Still nothing. I turned to look to the dog for reassurance. That pause put the pair of birds into the air. Spinning around I picked out a single. I was mounting the gun as I turned, and as I picked up the bird over the barrels, I noticed a big, fanned tail with a dark ban across it. Here was the ruffed grouse we searched for. It was an easy going away shot, and the grouse hung suspended for a moment before dropping stone dead onto the carpet of mottled aspen leaves. Ginny had the grouse and was returning with it as I broke the gun. As I gently placed the grouse in my game bag I turned to look back toward the truck. Something slapped me right in the face!

I was looking down on the field from where we entered this covert. I was on a little hill. Looking more carefully I realized I was in the middle of what looked like high ground. Not much higher than the rest but definitely higher. We had found the hills. We later discovered that what they called the hills in this section of Manitoba was land that might only be 50 feet above the rest of the land. Another observation was that the vegetation was different. More aspen, spruce and low, thick brush. That chance discovery of the hills that first year has paid off in hundreds of ruffed grouse flushes since.

And here we were again. The familiar old dirt road, the little rise in the land and off in the distance stood the ancient, gray, skeleton of a fire tower. This alone should have let us know we were in the highest country around. This entire area had apparently burned years ago creating vast openings separated by strips and islands of aspen and willow. To add character to the land there were the old, twisted spruce trees that for years had withstood the constant wind that roars down off lake Winnipeg. The country is so vast that there are no real boundaries. You can usually hunt until both you and the dog are dragging.

Our old friend George met us at the truck for lunch. After a hurried meal we were off again, now that we had found the hills. George would go off straight out along the road towards the fire tower. Jan chose to hunt along the edge where the field met the old timber. We would meet at dusk. Pixie and I headed off into a big hourglass shaped hay field. Along the edges were stands of mixed aged aspen. The understory of the cover was thick with willow, brush and charred remains of the timber that withstood the last fire. What a place to run dogs.

It was easy walking along the edge. Pixie was threading the edge of the field and the cover. She swung out into the field to skirt an island of aspen with some dead limbs scattered through it. I was about to cast her back into the thicker cover along the edge when she wheeled and pointed into the center of the low brush. As I worked into position I kept thinking this was pretty thin cover for ruffed grouse. Then I looked down and saw the glistening red and pink berries. Tea berries back home, but wintergreen in this part of the world.

I was still ten yards from the dog when they started out. Two ruffs came out together. I swung on the right hand one and mashed the trigger as the barrels of the 20 gauge S/S passed his head. He tumbled at the shot and I was already swinging on the other before the first hit the ground. I caught a flash of another, and then another going back to the right as I tracked the second one. It was a long shot but the modified barrel, like Ma Bell, reached out and touched him. He wasn't hit as hard as the first. Pixie dropped the first and raced after the second one. I broke the gun and caught the two empties as the ejectors kicked them out. Before I could reload another grouse came out of the far side of the little island. As I stuffed two more shells into the 20 two more thundered away towards the back of the field. I knelt as Pixie tried to pick up both grouse at the same time. She couldn't quite figure it out, and I walked over to help her.

Five minutes into the covert and I had a beautiful pair of Manitoba ruffs in the game bag. In the heat of the battle I had managed to keep track of the grouse that came out of that low, open cover. Seven birds. Probably a brood that hadn't been split up yet. Standing there admiring my brace of birds I could hear shots in the distance. George and Jan, both apparently finding grouse. The birds were back, maybe not in the previous numbers yet, but definitely back. What I am about to say will sound strange to a true grouse hunter, but it is true. Because of the low, thin cover the shooting is actually too easy. When there are birds it is no great feat to take a limit of five grouse if you shoot them as you come upon them. Because of this we decided long ago that we would shoot only birds the dogs handle well. There is no reason to do otherwise. Great land, this Manitoba, where a grouse is a grouse and where they wear both fantails and sharptails.

But for the hunter with dogs, there is much in Manitoba to enjoy, even when the birds are not at all-time highs. For those of us accustomed to rooting our grouse out of thickets of grape, thornapple, alder, and briers, and where a dog without a beeper or bell is lost half of the time, this open country is extremely inviting. Imagine hunting your grouse dogs without bells and beepers and having them in sight 90 percent of the time. Picture a dog locked on point in a thin stand of 15-foot high aspen and walking in to flush a flock of sharptails or a pair of ruffs from under the dog's nose. Watch them as they sail out across waist-high cover. The cover here is measured in miles not acres. Liberal bags, should you choose to fill them, await you. And the excitement, the anticipation, the tension as you walk in on a quivering dog on point. Will it be a pair of fantails or a flock of sharptails?

This is Manitoba, Mecca for the gunner with dogs.

Road to The Land of "Haws"

I couldn't get Dorothy, Toto and the Yellow Brick Road out of my mind as I followed the remains of a winding old logging road up and up for almost 20 minutes. I was carrying my vintage, 20 gauge, Browning O/U instead of an old broom. It wasn't a scruffy little mutt like Toto bouncing and slashing back and forth in front of me on one side of the road and then the other. No, it was Tinker, a lovely, little, liver and white Elhew pointer. And the road, it wasn't yellow brick but instead it was covered with multicolored leaves, tea berries and clover. We were on a journey in grouse country.

I had stopped to talk to the old man on his porch near Mt. Davis, the highest point in Pennsylvania, located in the southwestern part of the state. This is up tight against both West Virginia and Western Maryland. All three states are similar in this corner of the world. I was looking for old abandoned farms and new this old mountaineer had been around long enough to remember any that may be in the country.

We exchanged greetings and I got right to the point. Before I could get into my questions the old fellow beat me to the punch. He asked what type of dog that was in the truck, the white one with the long hair that had black patches and the small marks all over him. I explained that this was an English setter. He commented that he had never owned one like that but had one very similar that they used to work cows years ago. He said that his was a border collie and looked like my setter.

The sun was nearing the high mountain in the back ground and I wanted to get on with my search. Again, before I could pursue my questions, he went on to explain that while he never had a setter he had owned a short shorthaired hound like the brown and white one in the truck. It was one of the best fox hounds in the mountains he assured me. I told him mine was an English pointer, of the Elhew Kennel, but his only comment was to inquire as to how good it ran a fox. I tried to explain that it didn't but never really felt he believed me.

Finally I got around to asking where I might find an old abandoned farm that was growing back into brush. To be specific, I was looking for old pastures that were growing back into hawthorn and different types of young brush. He said that there was an old farm on the mountain and he remembered that many years ago it had a lot of crab apples. Crab apples are often what the local people call hawthorn. I was getting more excited by the moment. He pointed to the mountain with a callused hand, hardened from time and hard work. "There, where the saddle is cut into the mountain, that's where the old road ran." Follow it to the top and just over the top there used to be a vast pasture with those little red and yellow crab apples. He went on to say that the road was not passable by truck but I could walk up there in about 15 or 20 minutes.

It took a lot of faith as the only thing visible was big, dark, mature timber. I have faith in old people, and some day I hope to be one myself. Tinker was looking for the cover. She would be on one side then the other but it was all the same. There were some grapevines in the big timber but nothing that really looked like grouse cover. The road was winding and switching back and forth and I guess this was what made me think of Dorothy and the land of Oz.

As we rounded the next bend I could see a bright spot at the top of the road. It looked as if it would come into some sort of opening. We had about an hour and a half of good daylight, and for the grouse hunter that last hour is the best of the day. I knew if there were any grouse, they would be out feeding.

When we topped the last little rise the forest opened up into a virtual sea of old pastures that had long ago gone back to hawthorn. I couldn't believe my eyes. There, stretched for about a half mile, was a rolling vista dotted with gray, twisted hawthorn trees. Each one was a red tint with the fruit that still hung on even after the first few frosts.

Tinker saw it also and raced into the old fields, head high searching for scent. I hadn't quite reached the edge of the hawthorns when her bell fell silent. I looked to the left and there she stood, rooted to the ground, staring into a clump where two hawthorns had grown together. One had blown down but still had roots partially buried enough to produce fruit. I quickened my step, but before I had closed the gap to fifty yards a big old cock bird lifted from under the tangle. With tail fanned his chestnut band shone brightly in the late afternoon sun as he banked and pitched into the edge of the woods about a 100 yards farther ahead.

Tinker took a step or two and pointed again, only this time she was crouched low to the ground as if to spring. I had seen this before and knew that it meant she had a bird and he was close to her point. By now I was able to circle a little and was coming at her from the side. I had the bird between the dog and me. The 20 ga. Browning was at port arms in anticipation of the flush. Then I heard that peeping, guttural sound a grouse makes when trapped and not sure where to burst out.

The dog didn't move and when I looked into the tangle I saw the bird on the ground. She had her head stuck straight in the air and was running for all she was worth to get out from under the overhanging branches. I usually blow a shot like this. When I see them on the ground I seem to have too much time to get ready and with this false sense of too much time don't get into action soon enough.

This time was different. I was tracking the bird as the gun was coming up to my shoulder. The stock hit my shoulder at about the same time the grouse cleared the overhanging limbs and burst into full flight. He saw the dog and banked away from Tinker. I was swinging on him when he went behind another tree. I kept the gun swinging and was on him as he cleared the tree and broke into a little clearing, headed for the woods edge just as the other had done.

The little Browning was swinging smoothly and I passed his nose just before he got to the big timber. I hit the trigger and saw him go limp as the 1oz. charge of 8's hit him from the I.C. barrel. He folded without a flutter and slammed into the forest floor at the edge of the woods. Tinker had also been following his escape route and she was on him when he made his last flutter. It was another big old male, and when Tinker picked it up she got a wing over her right eye. She had a hard time finding my location but soon got it figured out. Here she came with this giant of a grouse, one wing covering her eye but head high and proud. We took a moment to admire his warm colors and tucked him into the game bag.

Tinker was off again with me walking the old road that meandered down through the hawthorn. It almost gave the impression of an orchard. The trees were in somewhat of a row pattern even though they were randomly spaced. Tinker was ahead and to the left. Her bell stopped and at the same moment I heard a grouse roar off, then another and then another until there were six in all that went out in front of her. I couldn't tell what happened so no need to give her hell. I can only think she caught them out feeding in the open and when she stopped they just began to get up.

The roar of each pair of wings was a signal to the next to get airborne. 15 minutes and we had moved eight different birds! I brought Tinker in and tried to calm her down a little before releasing her again. She knew there were birds out there and wasn't interested in being petted and told what a nice dog she was. All she had on her mind was grouse.

I found that we were skirting the edge of the cover and only hitting about a 1/4th. of it. But we were finding birds, and the hunting was easy. The little trail of a road went along the edge of the cover and I could walk it while the dog worked the unforgiving thorns of the hawthorn trees. The ground was covered with the fruit. One interesting thing was that we found both red haws as well as yellow ones.

I blew the whistle to bring Tinker in, and when I did, two grouse roared away to my right, smack dab in the middle of the covert. We had about 30 minutes of good daylight left and there would be no way to cover this vast expanse in such short time. I sent Tinker off into the direction where the last two headed and followed along on the old road.

She came to a little stand of goldenrod and jacked up into a point. Her nose was down some and her rear end up. The goldenrod had grown around a few trees where the soil was fertile from the rotting fruit building up over the years. I thought woodcock, but was prepared for grouse. I walked by her and nothing happened. She didn't move, no bird flushed and I just stood there. Searching the ground ahead of her I spotted a big dark eye. The woodcock's eye and mine came together at the same time and for a brief moment neither knew what to do. Before I could think of my next move the woodcock sprang into the air.

He twisted and darted as he cleared the first tree. I shot much too fast as the gun was already tracking the bird when he lifted off the ground. After the first shot the woodcock banked to the left and headed for the timber. It was long shot, but the mod. barrel hit him hard and sent him tumbling back to the dark earth. While some dogs refuse to retrieve a woodcock Tinker relishes the opportunity. She scooped it up without missing a step and rushed back to me.

She seemed to be saying "here, take this one while I find another before it gets too dark to hunt." The little russet fellow was tucked carefully into the game bag. I hate to ruffle the feathers of a game bird, only to haul it out at the end of the day and not be able to tell which end is which. Things of beauty in death, just as they were in life, we owe them a certain respect.

The old road made another bend to the left and headed into the middle of this ocean of grouse cover. Tinker was off again and was on her way back towards me when she pulled up in one of her high headed points. I was looking right at her this time and could see the bulging of the eyes and the flaring of the nostrils as she gathered in that wonderful aroma. Here one of the old hawthorn trees had blown over and up through it grew greenbrier berries. I knew we had this bird dead to right.

He was pinned between me and the dog. I was walking silently along the road and Tinker was coming at him from behind. As I neared the dog she seemed to get bigger, as if she were swelling up. She was very high on both ends, almost standing on her toes. She was getting a nose full for sure. I was about twenty yards from her when I caught some movement in the tangle of briers and limbs. Peering in between the branches I spotted a hen grouse walking out from the fallen tree trunk right towards me, flicking her tail as she came.

It is unusual to see so many grouse before they take flight, and it usually only happens when there has been very little hunting pressure. I decided later that was the case with this particular covert. When she reached the crown of the fallen tree she roared into the air in a swirl of leaves and twigs. It was open though and she decided to cross the road and head towards the big woods. She never made it as a fast swing overtook her. Such a fast swing takes very little lead and it almost looked as if I was shooting right at her when the gun went off. In reality a fast swing often takes you beyond the target before you can stop yourself, giving you the right lead automatically. The charge of 8's hit her hard and she pitched right into the grass at the edge of the old road.

Tinker brought the grouse and we stopped for a moment to look it over and let her nuzzle it for the last time before tucking it into the game bag. We had our two bird limit now and the sun was about ready to set. As we turned we were looking directly into the sun, three fourths hidden by big, black Mt. Davis. As if painted there, the remaining sun just happened to be in the middle of the old road we were following back out of this covert.

I looked at Tinker and told her that she was a great dog. She seemed to understand and got up tight against my left leg. I told her that she was a much better dog than Toto and even though we hadn't discovered the Road Into The Land Of Oz, we certainly found The Road Into the Land Of "Haws." The wonderful thing about the haws country is that it changes so little over the years. Once the hawthorn takes over a pasture it only seems to get better. More trees come and with them more grouse and woodcock.

We stopped to thank the old man again for his information as we left the mountain. That was several years ago and I hunt the covert still today. The old man is gone now but every time I pass the house I can still see him sitting there, pointing with those long, thin, crooked fingers. "There, up there where the saddle is in the mountain. Take your dogs up there and you will find an old farm and those crab apples you are looking for. Just follow what is left of the old road!"

"Pops" and The Revised Road Hunting Technique

If you read "Of Guns and Dogs and Men" you will no doubt remember the sections on my dear friend, and mentor, George Burroughs. No book of mine on ruffed grouse, bird hunting, and bird dogs would be complete without detailing the experiences of this unique individual. Truly the Big Man broke the mold after he made George. In his early 80's, he still remains the most enthusiastic and dedicated bird hunter and bird dog man I have yet to meet.

He has one of the most optimistic views of life I have yet to run across. As mentioned, he is in his early 80's and we are planning a breeding for my Elhew pointer so we will have breeding stock ten years from now when we each need a fresh pup. I knew one other man who had George's optimistic outlook on life. He was French Queen. Unlike George, French didn't take his pleasure in hunting; he took it in making money and owning property. He once told me that he had just finalized a great deal that morning. It seemed he had leased a piece of property to a man who wanted to build a barn on the property. The deal was that the man had the lease of the property for 20 years. After 20 years, the property would revert back to French along with any improvements. French was delighted with the deal he made that morning. He was 87 at the time!

In the fall of '95 his burning passion for grouse hunting and working his beloved Elhew pointers may have reached a milestone. George had found a vast expanse of prime grouse country up in Ontario the year before. He had explored it, hunted it, made contacts and thoroughly enjoyed his new-found treasure. Concerned with his well- being, we had all mentioned to George that he should not hunt this vast wilderness alone. No one tells George what to do, we just suggest many different options and let him pick the one that best suits his plans.

Anyway, George decided it might be nice to have company on an extended trip to open the season in Canada. It just so happened that during this period a nice young man came into the picture and struck up a relationship with George. He assured George that he too was a dedicated grouse hunter.

Tomba skirts an edge where islands of young aspen ooze out into grown-up pastures of wintergreen and clover. This is ideal cover where fantails and sharptails overlap.

He had no dogs and would love to go with George into this country running over with grouse. So it came to pass that the young man accompanied George on the trek north.

Those of us who know George love and respect him. We understand his love of his dogs and what a big part they play in his life. They travel as would any of George's friends, in the passenger compartment of his Range Rover. He usually has four to six, and on this particular trip I think he had five. The pointers have long ago worked out the seating arrangements in the Range Rover. The top dog usually sits in the front passenger seat. If another hunter rides with George, the Top Dog resigns himself to the position of back seat with head handing over the shoulder of the passenger. Occasionally there may be a little drooling, but that is what dogs do.

Two will usually take a back window apiece and one of the young ones, who has motion sickness, buries his head in a rear corner, never to look up until the vehicle stops. Since they eat, sleep, travel and live in the Range Rover it sometimes takes on a fragrance somewhat hostile to the unaccustomed. This lifestyle was a little different, to say the least, for the young sophisticated hunter. So, in September, George, his troupe of pointers, and the young hunter headed north.

With visions of flushing grouse blocking out the sun the young man was able to at least tolerate the dogs. I am sure that was the longest 18 hour drive he ever endured as he survived the occasional growling, snapping and drooling. He even learned to breathe without taking in air as the five dogs passed a little gas. Like a true grouse hunter he was taking it in stride but developing a definite intolerance as the trip progressed.

Finally they arrived in far western Ontario and were able to pile out of the Range Rover. The new-found freedom was enjoyed by all. This section of Canada is crisscrossed by countless logging roads, sandy and relatively smooth. Also this country is sparsely populated. Throw all this in a pot and add numerous grouse, and you have an ideal hunting and training situation.

George is never finished training a dog. He is always striving for more from his dogs and never tires of the search and the work. With his new-found friend, George had planned to divide up the dogs and each would work a dog or two at a time. It was at this juncture that George began to realize that all might not be as he thought it was. As they traveled the old roads the first couple of days they saw several grouse taking gravel at road's edge. It was becoming more difficult for the young hunter as they passed each sitting bird. Finally he couldn't take it any longer and asked George to let him out, and he would try to flush some of them and shoot them.

Of course, George preferred to hunt the edges with his dogs and take the birds as the dogs pointed and held for the flush. Without the involvement of the dogs George simply doesn't consider it grouse hunting. If it weren't for the dogs George wouldn't be out there at all. Without the dog work it becomes grouse shooting, or killing, and not hunting.

But being the gentleman that he is George agreed to let the young hunter try his own style of hunting. As George watched the fellow tiptoed up to grouse as they sat feeding and taking gravel. Needless to say he shot several, and some, I think, were flying! George allows everyone their freedom of thought and action. Even though this was the farthest thing from what George considers grouse hunting, he never mentioned it.

Well, the small cabin they shared was getting smaller by the day. Five dogs and two hunters was about all that it could handle. Not all of the dogs were completely house broken, and occasionally an accident was sure to happen. It did a time or two too many for the young hunter. George could notice a definite change as the young fellow became more sullen and removed. George even thought he could hear the fellow talking to himself. He appeared to have a lost look in his eyes. I think it was the third night, or maybe the fourth, when things began to fall apart.

After all day in the coverts, a day where few grouse were found, they returned to the shrinking cabin. The dogs seemed a little more irritable than usual. They get that way when they hunt hard. While they had long ago worked out the seating arrangements in the Range Rover they were still experimenting with the sleeping arrangements of the cabin. Until that time nothing completely agreeable to all five had been found.

Somewhere between the feeding and sleeping arrangements things got a little out of hand. Quick as a flushing grouse, all five dogs tore into each other. It was a melee of unbelievable proportions, a true Boone and Crockett dog fight! Heads, tails and fur going in all directions. George was wading into the swirl of pointers pulling, grabbing and swatting with his lead strap, all to no avail.

In looking for something to break up the free for all he was glancing around the room when he spotted the young fellow in a corner. The young hunter's eyes were as big as coffee cups and he was much whiter than he had seemed at dinner. The blood curdling fight was still raging when George finally found what he was looking for, a can of Mace he kept in his duffel. Immediately he waded back into the wad of dogs and began to spray everything that moved. Not moving is probably what saved the young hunter from a shot of mace. That was all it took and things quickly returned to the calm serenity a northwoods cabin is so famous for.

George resumed the task of finishing his dinner but it was several minutes before his companion came forward from the corner. He eased into the one stuffed chair in the cabin and sort of collapsed. In a few minutes he seemed to tense up and a strange expression came across his face. As George watched, the fellow seemed to be working his nose, the way a pointing dog does when trying to locate scent. While working his nose the young fellow was slowly easing back out of the chair, rising in a sort of a corkscrew fashion as if trying to see where he had been while trying to go somewhere else. Then he let out a noise, somewhere between a scream and a shriek!

Some time during the previous free-for-all one of the dogs had apparently taken the time, before jumping into the melee, to mark his spot with a rather loose bowel movement. George was helping with the clean up of the chair and his companion's hunting pants, but for some reason the fellow didn't seem overly appreciative. The cleanup complete, things returned to normal, whatever normal is when George is around. It was decided that the dogs should sleep in the Range Rover that night as sort of a punishment for the bad behavior in the cabin.

As they were led out of the cabin George noticed a sort of smirk on the face of young Buck, the current top dog of the crew. George couldn't really pin it down but Buck was looking back over his shoulder straight at the young hunter as if it were his fault that they had to leave the warmth of the cozy cabin. Sleep came easy that night as all seemed exhausted from the excitement of the day.

The morning dawned clear, fresh and promising. Lunches packed, maps tucked away, guns and shells gathered George and his companion went outside to the Range Rover. After it was all over George remembered it seemed strange that top dog wasn't sitting in the front passenger seat. All five were sitting on the back seat watching as the two hunters entered the auto. George's companion plopped down in the passenger seat, ready to go again. As George slid under the wheel, he glanced over to see the same nose-twitching, slow motion seat exit he had seen the young man execute the night before in the cabin.

Well, you guessed it. One of the dogs, no way to tell for sure which one, figuring it was the young fellows fault he had to sleep in the cold car instead of the warm cabin, again marked his spot with a fresh, soft BM! George's offers to help with the clean- up went unheard. The young man told George not to waste his hunting time helping with the clean up. Instead he told George to come back and get him at lunch time, and they could hunt together that afternoon.

George enjoyed the morning, not having to stop while the other hunter tried to sneak up on the sitting birds, but felt guilty about having such a great morning while his buddy was at the cabin waiting for him. George cut his hunt short and returned to get the young hunter. But the strangest thing had happened. The people who owned the cabin said that as soon as George had pulled out of sight the young fellow had asked them to take him to town where he had caught the first bus south, no where in particular, just south back toward Michigan. It seemed he had an emergency come up and had to return. Words can't describe how bad George felt for the poor fellow. He felt that the hunt might not have been going as smoothly as his new companion would have hoped and now to have such a great trip cut short! Well there is always next year.

As mentioned earlier there is no more enthusiastic and dedicated hunter than George. He found himself alone with two weeks of his three week trip remaining. In his 80's, and with a hip problem, he had devised a way of giving hunting time to all of his dogs. He had seen the top trainers work dogs off horse back and even four wheelers. He had trained his dogs to hunt the edges of these old roads while he followed slowly in the Range Rover. He would get out, uncase his gun, approach the pointing dog and take the shot if it presented itself. If the bird flushed, presenting no shot, it made no real difference to George as it was all for the dogs anyway.

Undaunted by the rapid retreat, or should we say getaway, of his hunting buddy George set about to work and hunt his dogs two at a time. The country here lends itself perfectly to this type of hunting. There are wide strips of cover along the old roads and they are rough enough that people don't come flying along. Besides there are few people and very few cars that are not hunters. The rest of the week went well. George and the dogs were finding birds and all of the dogs were getting plenty of work. He was shooting one to two grouse per day and this was plenty for him.

During the third week a couple of the younger dogs were getting their confidence in the strange country and reaching a bit farther. George believes in letting them run when they are young. Occasionally they would get out ahead of him where there was a bend in the road and disappear in the brush. Slowing and blowing the horn always brought them back to the road. Well, almost always. The two young dogs were out hunting ahead of the white Range Rover and feeling their oats. He believes it builds confidence and the hunting spirit.

George slowed a little and began to blow the horn as the dogs rounded a bend in the road. He would wait on this side of the bend, with the idea that the dogs would come to the road, not see him, get a little scared and race back to their master. What is it they say about, men, mice and plans?

As he slowed he heard something behind him. Looking in the mirror he saw a white station wagon coming up fast. It went on around him before he could really think of what might happen. At that point Murphy's Law went into effect. He sat there a moment or two blowing the horn of his white

Range Rover but the dogs didn't come racing back around the bend to him. Then it struck him. White Range Rover, white station wagon!

He went on around the bend and still didn't see the dogs or the white wagon. What he did see was a "Y" in the road. Now what? Well, the Good Lord looks after good people and their dogs, and he was watching out for my friend George. George took the right fork and in a minute or two came upon the white wagon. In front of the white wagon were two pointers running for all they were worth to stay ahead of it.

George began to blow the horn. The fellow ahead unknowingly thought he was going too slow, speeded up, and the dogs ran faster, widening the gap between them and George.

I think you have to stop here for a moment to get this picture in your mind. Here goes this little caravan of white wagons. The dogs are ahead, George is behind, and in between is a fellow who has no idea what is going on. The dogs know they are supposed to hunt ahead of the white wagon and are doing all they can to stay ahead. Finally they tire a little and the front auto shoots on by. Now they think George is leaving them! On around the bend they go in hot pursuit of the white wagon. It speeds up, they speed up, and George speeds up blowing his horn all the while. The dogs are being left behind, and they have someone behind them blowing the horn telling them to go faster.

Well, this went on for another mile or two before the dogs stop to size up the situation. George said he honestly thinks he saw first bewilderment, and then, a smile across their faces when they saw him in the white Range Rover with their litter mates.

Not to know George is not to experience some of the greatest of joys this thing called bird hunting has given us. I count very lucky indeed the day he took me under his wing. There will never be another!

CHAPTER 3

THE SCHOOL BUS STOP

It was December, right after deer season. This has traditionally been a time when I learn of new grouse coverts. With so many deer hunters in the woods a few always run into groups of grouse. The secret is to be able to sort the fact from the B.S. Unless you are a true bird hunter it is very difficult to accurately judge the number of birds you have moved. I have been able to sort it out pretty well over the years. I guess the old saying of "it takes one to know one" may be the secret.

Jack had hunted the big cover behind the School Bus Stop two days during the deer season and told me that he had jumped at least 25 or 30 grouse. Jack and I had hunted together for a couple of years back then and I knew he could be counted on for accurate counts of grouse moved. We agreed to go back once the deer season was over. Just when I thought the deer season would never end it did. The following Saturday found us pulled in against the school bus stop. Being Saturday we weren't blocking the bus and this was basically the only place to get off the road.

Jack was going through that stage we have all been through. He was searching for that magic gun, the one that fit perfectly, was self pointing, light to carry and a joy to own. At this time he was trying a short, light over and under made by Franchi. It was supposed to be the great bird gun of the century. It had 24 inch barrels and for me seemed much to choppy, to stiff and jerky. It had no symmetry, no grace and lacked that thing we call *feel*. It simply didn't feel alive. Anyway, Jack was carrying it as I uncased my Parker V grade 16 gauge. Jack's dad, Vaughn, was carrying his time-tested 16 gauge model 12.

We hit the bank behind the bus stop and started up through the timber. Sally, our English setter was searching for the cover that was not yet in sight. Jack assured me that, as soon as we hit the bench above the flat we were on, we would be into some great cover.

We pushed ahead following the little setter who was slashing back and forth trying to hunt in front of all three of us. Sally reached the bench before we did and her bell went silent. I signaled to Vaughn and Jack to move up to the brink of the bank as Sally must be on point. The three of us marched forward in a spaced line with guns at the ready. We topped the bank and I saw Sally stretched as stiff as a poker about 50 yards ahead. She was pointing into a clump of greenbrier that had grown around a tangle of grape vines and dogwood.

From her intensity I knew she had the grouse nailed. Wanting Jack and Vaughn to get the shot I told them to get ready and I would go in to flush the bird. I knew how bad Jack wanted to try that new gun on grouse. It had the barrel selector on the safety like many other over unders. You had to shove it over and then up to fire. I eased up to Sally and, just as I started to tell Jack to get ready, the grouse exploded off the forest floor. There was a swirl of leaves where the bird was and I was tracking its flight as it hooked back towards Jack. He would have a perfect shot as the grouse climbed for altitude.

He was tracking the bird and taking plenty of time like he should. We always seem to shoot too quickly. I was watching and waiting for the report. The bird kept hooking and was in front of Jack now. Now it was to the side, and now it was gone! I looked to Jack to see him staring down at his great new grouse gun. "No shot?" I asked, trying to give him an excuse to use. "I had the perfect shot," he said. "The bird was just hooking and hanging in front of me as if suspended in time, he looked like he was moving in slow motion." Vaughn chipped in that he didn't try the shot because he was waiting for Jack to drop it.

Jack is not one to make excuses or to be over talkative. His only comment was that he must have jammed the safety in the middle position. This prevented the gun from firing either barrel. Problem solved we headed on around the side of the hill. Here the cover was thin and scattered clumps of locust, greenbrier, dogwood and hawthorn lay before us. We hadn't gone 100 yards when Sally slammed into another point. This time she was looking straight down hill towards Vaughn. He was on the outside and was ready as Jack went in.

I was ready and Vaughn was as tight as a cocked steel trap. The grouse came out in front of me and went towards Vaughn. I saw the bird explode before I heard the shot. Sally went to the bird, picked it up, spit it out and stood there pawing at her mouth which was covered with loose feathers. I picked up what was left of the grouse and handed the remains to Vaughn. "Little quick weren't you, " I asked Vaughn. He pointed out that he felt sure that in another instant the grouse would have been swallowed up by the cover. As I checked his model 12, I found that it was a full choke. No wonder the bird had exploded when he centered it with a charge of high base 6's.

Sally was off again with us following. There was a stretch between the covert we were in and a big hollow ahead, separated by a narrow neck of cover comprised of locust and briers. These thorns were the most fierce looking I have ever seen. Jack told me they were Honey Locust trees. I felt that a dog could be killed if it ran into one of these trees. They surely must have been the thorns that made up the crown that Christ wore to his crucifixion.

I am not sure what the grouse were feeding on, but they were in there thick. Instead of one or two going out in front of Sally's point it was often three or four. The shooting was good and we were each killing a bird now and then. Every now and then I would hear Jack say something that would reflect on his gun's mother. Every now and then he would get a perfect shot, wide open and with plenty of time to get on the bird. He was still having the safety problem. All the while Vaughn and I were adding to our game bags.

There were birds in every piece of good looking cover. It was one of the most exciting hunts we ever had. Sally was in her prime and she was working those birds with one solid find after another. We alternated shots, with Vaughn and I taking ours, while Jack fought his new grouse gun.

We had worked our way back into the corner of the covert now and the grouse were thundering away at regular intervals. I could see that Jack was very frustrated and knew that his ownership of this great grouse gun was to be short lived. We were hunting along the top of an old strip job now and the flat dropped sharply over the highwall. We had taken nine grouse between us at this point. Vaughn and I had taken our four bird limit and Jack had one.

I was working the dog and enjoying this great experience while Vaughn was simply caught up in the excitement and pleasure of watching a great grouse dog work her birds. We would soon reach the end of the covert and had planned to cut back through a big pasture. This meant that we had about another 50 yards to hunt and this memorable day would be over. Sure enough we were almost at the end when Sally locked up again looking into a big tangle where a fallen tree was laced with grapevines. Jack was ready and I walked in to flush the bird.

Some may say why didn't he take his safety off before the bird flushed, but most will understand that we never take the safety off until we are in the motion of mounting the gun. This would be the last shot of the day and I could tell that Jack wanted this grouse. I could see his white knuckles glowing in the shadows of the dark hollow as he squeezed the life out of the grip of the gun. He was in perfect position and I went in to put the bird in the air.

I walked up to Sally but nothing happened. She was so intense there was no question she had her bird pinned. I told Jack this as I moved past her nose. Still nothing! I kept going and was about ten steps in front of the dog when we heard wings beating the brush as the bird fought for altitude. It seemed like 10 seconds before the big red grouse broke free of the greenbrier. Jack had plenty of time and I knew he would center this grouse as it reached for the safety of the thicket on the hill. But he didn't.

No shot, no falling bird and nothing for Sally to retrieve. Well not really. As I looked to Jack I saw him break the gun open, remove the shells and close it again. I thought he was going to put it over his arm and start for home. I guess he had all he could take. Jack was not prone to curse but this would make a preacher swear. We had recorded 42 flushes in about four hours of hunting, Vaughn and I had taken limits of grouse over solid points and Jack had spent one very frustrated day.

As I turned to head out of the covert I heard a little commotion and turned in time to hear a comment about the mother of the gun, and something about the gun having no father. Next I saw Jack hurl the thing over the high wall. It stuck, barrels first in the soft mud. We discussed the actions for a moment and Vaughn pointed out that $400 was quite a chunk to throw over the hill no matter how mad you were. Jack knew it was the wrong thing to do but he was so frustrated at the miserable safety that he felt it was a living thing and had to be punished. The gun was retrieved and we headed back out of the School Bus Covert.

We knew we had found a real bonanza in this covert and couldn't wait to get back. It was about two weeks later before Jack and I returned to the School Bus Stop covert again. This time Jack had his 16gauge Fox Sterlingworth and we had high hopes for another glorious day in the grouse. As we started up the bank again we were discussing the color of the sky. It was mid December now and the sky was very threatening. They weren't calling for any snow but it sure looked dark.

The author and Tomba stop for a moment with the spine of the Appalachians sprawling away below them.

We were two hours from the truck and didn't really relish the idea of getting out of there soaking wet and cold. We began to trace our steps of the last hunt. Sure enough, Sally hit the hillside above the bus stop and didn't go 100 yards before hitting a solid point. I knew how bad Jack wanted to shoot that bird and told him to get ready while I went in to flush it. He needed it, as a confidence builder if nothing else, after the fiasco with the Franchi O/U on the last hunt. Sally was rock solid and I began a circle to put the grouse between me, Jack and Sally.

I was in good position now if the bird broke my way instead of going back over Jack. One, two, three steps but no flush. Sally never blinked. I glanced at Jack and all I could see was white knuckles and clenched teeth. He had a death grip on that old Fox and I knew that If the grouse didn't flush soon his hands would go to sleep and he wouldn't be able to get the safety off. He was as tight as a banjo string. I went another step and still nothing. Sally was fixed on a little pile of logs in front of her that had some greenbrier and grape vine sewed into it.

I felt sure the bird was behind the log but wondered why it sat so tight. As much confidence as I had in Sally, I have to admit I was starting to doubt her. I even tried to cluck her on. Sometimes on a running grouse I could make her move up a little even before she was ready. Not this time. She was glued to the spot. "He's in here Jack, " I said. "You get ready. I am going to bust into that clump of brush and put him out."

If you have ever tried to bulldog your way through multiflora rose, greenbrier and grapevine cover you will understand the next few seconds. I tucked my head down and took a step forward. A greenbrier hooked me around the left foot. I made a half lunge to free myself and, when I did, a big old multiflora rose thorn hooked into the side of my nose. That stopped the progress for a second. You simply don't bull your way on forward when a wild rose thorn has you by the nose. I tried to ease back a step but got tangled in the grapevines. I started to fall backwards but managed to lunge forward again and in so doing pitched right over the little pile of logs. There staring me in the face was a big old cock grouse.

I was draped over the log as he took a few quick steps to get out from the tangle. In a flash he was roaring away. I guess all the commotion had distracted him from realizing Jack was still there. The grouse went out to the right in front of Jack, and then seeing him went the only place he could, straight away and up. I saw the whole scene from my back, the tucked feet and the tilt of the tail as he changed directions, and the impact of the shot.

At the right distance, Jack hit him hard with a load of Remington Surshot from the right barrel of the Fox. The bird was centered with the pattern and was dead in the air. I could see a little smile of satisfaction come over Jack as he took the bird from Sally. Then a burst of laughter as he sized up my plight. When I finally got untangled he mentioned that my fall was the longest he had ever witnessed.

He said I fell for about 20 feet with a hop, skip and a jump and it took about ten seconds to accomplish. In addition I may need a transfusion before he got me out of the woods. Something about the briers that make you bleed! But all in all it had been worth it and a great start to the day. We continued to trace our steps and found one grouse after another.

It was darker now than I had ever seen it at 2:00 in the afternoon. I remember discussing the fact that the sky now had the same greenish black cast that it did when we were kids and the Shinnston tornado struck, killing over 400 people. Sally was off again and when we rounded a little shoulder in the hill there she stood, a white statue against thc drab browns and grays of this dark, wet covert.

We saw her at the same time and began to move quickly and quietly towards her. This bird we didn't have to kick out. We were still 20 yards from the dog when the grouse had enough. Out it came and up the hill in front of me. It was the perfect low house no. 4. I don't remember swinging as it all happens so fast in this situation you rarely recall seeing the bead, the barrels or the lead. I must have been swinging fast because it seemed as if I shot right at the grouse. The bird slammed into the bank hard and flopped a few feet back towards me. Sally had it and in a few seconds brought it to my hand.

For the next hour the two scenes already described here were repeated several times. Some we got to and some flushed wild. Some we shot and many we missed. Above all we had four grouse when we got to the head of the hollow where the gun had been thrown over the highwall. The limit was four each and we were talking of taking no more from this cover. With those today and those of the last hunt we had enough, and were leaving several for seed. We agreed that we had a great day and that was enough.

Then Greed took over. While we were standing there, Sally was hunting as usual; she didn't understand limits or enough. All she ever knew was to hunt her heart out and find every bird in a piece of cover.

The wind began to pick up and it was almost dark even though it was now 3:00 PM. We started for the truck when Jack asked where Sally was. We began to look around and there, about 75 yards away, on the other side of an old split-rail fence she stood. Now we could have just flushed the grouse and let it go, like we have many times since that day and still had a great day.

But we were full of youth and exuberance and back then A LIMIT seemed to mean something. We loaded our guns and started back to the dog. We got to the fence at the same time and stepped over. What happened next is hard to explain, and really I have no explanation for what we did.

Our feet hit the ground at about the same time, and at the same time our feet hit the ground a clap of thunder and a bolt of lightning struck close by hard enough to shake us both. In an instant we turned, said nothing to each other but stepped back over the fence and started for the truck. Seconds after the thunder and lightning the hardest snow storm I have ever seen hit the head of the hollow. We were about 100 yards from the fence when Jack stopped and asked about Sally.

I turned to whistle for her and almost stepped on her. She was at my feet, tail tucked up tight against her stomach, and how she got there I have no idea. I want to think that the noise flushed the grouse and she simply followed Jack and I out of the hollow. We said very little until back to the truck. And then one of us made the comment that maybe the Big Man was watching the head of the hollow, remembered the cursing Jack had given the gun last week, and felt that he had given us a great day without that last grouse. Whatever it was it sent us out of the hollow with no questions asked and no explanations that we can give to this day. Mysteries abound in these old hollows down in Appalachia.

The Blue House

There will always be coverts that remain suspended in time. They have carried their character, their mystic and their lore through countless years. I have walked through these coverts and they draw me back now, even after 25 years. For various reasons they have remained the same. While the surrounding cover has grown out of what we call grouse cover and into turkey country, these isolated pockets are the constants in our lives year after year. While others betray us, these special, almost hallowed coverts have seen me through several lows of the cycle. One of my most treasured spots will remain "The Blue House."

It was November, 1970. While parts of Appalachia were struggling through a low cycle, there remained in Central West Virginia true honey holes. John Hart and I had hunted a favorite cover in the morning and had moved enough grouse to have been satisfied for the day. We decided to run into Weston, grab a sandwich and stop at Dave's Sport Shop so John could grab a box of low brass loads. Dave's was the gathering spot for all hunters in the area. During that time, there were few true grouse hunters and even fewer grouse dogs.

At Dave's, the talk soon turned to grouse and I inquired if any of the squirrel hunters or rabbit hunters had mentioned jumping any grouse lately. Dave motioned to a quiet young man standing in the corner. He said that Jack was in the woods about as much as anyone in the county, and if anyone knew if there were any grouse anywhere he would. Soon a conversation was struck and a friendship ignited between Jack Barnette and myself that gets stronger as I write this account of that first meeting. Jack was a quiet and deliberate man. I could tell from the beginning that he was one who could be believed.

Jack said that if we wanted to move some grouse that afternoon we should go to a certain hollow, drive to the end, park, take up over the strip job, climb the high wall, and be careful while doing it and head around the big point of the hill. His next statement brought my first doubts. "Hunt to the left first and then up over the top, there are around 15 or 16 grouse there in the grape vines." He said it with such certainty and matter of fact that while I had great doubts about the numbers I felt it was definitely worth checking. John and I discussed the account as we headed down the road. As I recall, we both had a small chuckle when we talked about all the grouse we were going to move. But the last laugh was to go to Jack.

We parked at the end of the dirt road, went up over the strip job and climbed the high wall. We stopped for a moment at the edge of the briers and grape vines to catch our breath. My English setter Sally went by us and into the cover. Before we realized it, her bell fell silent. We started into the cover and heard a grouse roar out, then another. John swung on the second and hit it with a load of 7 1/2's. Two grouse in about two minutes into the cover. We continued on around to the left and then up over the top.

It was up over the top that brought us into a time gone by. There, covered with living vines of grape, ivy and multiflora rose, stood a ghost of a house. There are many old, abandoned houses scattered throughout Central West Virginia and most of Appalachia. But there are none that are as BLUE as the blue house that still stands guard of this covert. It was the most brilliant, vivid blue I had ever seen. From its architecture, I guessed the house was built in the early 1900's. Look as I might I could see no reason why it was built so high on the mountain. There was no farm land near, no orchard and nothing to show that this person had any means of making a living here. I finally concluded that this must surely be the house of a true moonshiner. I could visualize him coming down in the still of the darkest night and bringing his corn squeezings into Weston, Buckhannon and even Clarksburg.

On both sides of the ridge, and all around the house, were tangles of grape vines and briers laced throughout the few mature trees that remained after the first cutting of the timber in the area. The land had been stripped for its coal but the seam ran around the mountain and left the top untouched. I can only imagine that this old mountaineer had to vacate when the strippers moved in. Or maybe the government men finally caught up with him. In any event, he was long gone.

What he left behind was one of the greatest pieces of grouse cover that I have ever followed the dogs through. Because of its makeup, the thick grape cover has continued to hold grouse in good numbers for nearly 25 years. Jack and I would hunt The Blue House at least two or three times a year during all those years, usually once a month. In all those years we never encountered another Grouse Hunter!

And how many grouse did we find that first afternoon? No, we didn't find 16 grouse as Jack said we would. As near as we could keep count, during the heat of the battle that ensued that first afternoon, we moved 14 different grouse. I don't know of anyone who ever called it any truer, or closer, than did Jack that first afternoon. And that accurate account of birds in the covert is what cemented our friendship so long ago. It was rare back then, and even rarer today, to find anyone who could give a true and accurate count of birds moved. Most hunters have no idea of the numbers and usually highly exaggerate the numbers.

Good food sources, good winter cover, enough natural openings in the woods to bring off broods and the lack of hunting pressure has given us a covert that we can count on year in and year out to provide a memorable hunt. No, the grouse don't show up in great numbers every year when they are nonexistent in other coverts, but even then there will be two and three times the numbers that the surrounding country contains.

We have trained and hunted three generations of setters at The Blue House. It can't be seen from any road and it hides it treasures on the back side and up over the top. And maybe that is exactly why it is built where it is. Maybe that is why it has never really been stripped and raped as most of these old houses have. If you read Of Guns and Dogs and Men you may realize that it was here that "Rock" went over the highwall, never to stand his grouse again after that terrible experience of a fifty foot free-fall.

But the good memories far outweigh the bad ones. I can still see Vaughn Barnette peering under the vines trying to spot the grouse that Sally had

Tomba stands his grouse in a grape tangle near the Blue House.

pinned. This was one of Vaughn's first hunts with a pointing dog and he had not yet overcome the urge to take them when and where he could. He fully understood that once in the air it was a completely different game. He soon realized that putting them into the air was the only game, and as far as I know he never shot another on the ground.

I only took one other person to that covert and that was Peppy, my hunting buddy and owner of Rock. Peppy quit hunting in later life and I never took another. Even though it was Jack's covert he felt obligated not to take anyone else there since he had shown it to me. He felt, and feels today, that this was our covert to hunt alone or with each other but never with a stranger. He feared, as I do, that few, if any, would respect this special covert as we do. The Blue House still stands, the grouse are still there and, oh yes, it is still very Blue.

CHAPTER 4

THE FRUITS OF FALL, HARVEST OF THE EASTERN GROUSE HUNTER

Something happens in the eastern grouse range with the first rains of August. The gunner with pointing dogs has suffered through the summer's heat. He has cleaned the kennels, fed the dogs, fought the mosquitoes, and cut the grass, but experience has shown that with the first rains of August the air will change. The gunner and the dogs will start to step a little higher and a little quicker.

The Kansas farmer will start to take off his milo and soybean crop and the quail hunter will be watching to see how the harvest goes. Farther west, in Montana, the farmers will be trying to get the wheat in while it is at maximum dryness. Those who follow their pointing dogs across those great expanses of The High Plains in search of the huns will be hoping that the crops were good and the harvest on time.

Along the spine of the Appalachians those rugged gunners with their tough pointing dogs are after a more self sufficient bird, one not so dependent on his neighbors the farmers. The ruffed grouse could care less if the corn is dry, picked or standing from the Carolinas up the Appalachian Chain and into New England He knows it is Mother Nature and the Good Lord's bounty that will see him through the harsh winter. While his northern cousins are dependent on the aspen for both cover and food the grouse of the Appalachians is more concerned with THE FRUITS OF FALL.

Those who roam the high, desolate coverts along the Appalachians know that frost comes early here and with it comes the first harvest of the fruits of fall. At every high mountain pasture, or SODS as they are known locally by the mountaineers who live there, splashes of color appear on the hawthorn.

Known as haws, thornapples, red or yellow haws, the hawthorn is the first fruit of significance to the grouse hunter and his dogs.

As we crossed Stony River and headed for Mount Storm, the colors of early fall were everywhere. The reds of the maples were brilliant, the yellows of the poplars were stunning, but it was the hawthorn that caught our eye. Scattered about in the old mountain pasture, along a strip of cut over timber the gray bark of the hawthorn was the perfect backdrop for the reds and yellows of the haws. It was plain to see that the haws had hit heavy. These old pastures are scattered all across the northern Appalachians and we knew if there was a grouse on the mountain he would be in the haws.

Pulling into a little clearing we stopped about 50 yards from a small clump of haws heavy with fruit. The early frost of the high country knocks them off and I believe the grouse can hear them hit the ground. Jack and I stepped out of the truck to stretch and he slammed his door. At that noise a pair of beautiful red phase ruffs roared away low from under the closest tree. Jack and I turned to each other with smiles of approval. Grouse in the open and scattered haws are a treat for both gunner and pointing dogs alike. The cover is sticky and unforgiving but it is open with very few leaves once the frost hits. The birds will often hold well when they are in the haws feeding.

Bells on the dogs, shells in the vests and the dogs were cut loose. I was hunting Tomba, our setter, and Tinker, our young Elhew pointer. Both were alive and animated in the cool mountain air. We worked into the general direction of the pair we flushed earlier as this was where we wanted to go anyway.

We had just entered the heart of the cover when I saw Tomba coming in from the left. I was watching as he flowed over the ground with the grace of a ballerina. Just as he passed a low growing hawthorn he spun around in a solid point. In the same moment Tinker saw him and went into one of her intense backs. I motioned "point" to Jack and he drifted over towards the dogs. He signaled for me to take the shot if one was presented as he moved on in for the flush. He was just about even with the setter when I heard the wings start.

The bird was against the tree and had to come out low to clear the thorny branches. As he cleared the lowest branch he hooked to the right and skyrocketed towards the heavier timber. He was trying to top out when the one ounce load of 7 1/2's hit him hard. It was a good shot and for just a moment he hung suspended against the bluest of October skies. He came back to earth through a hawthorn tree in a shower of the tiny apples. As I took the bird from Tomba I remember thinking that the fallen fruit would be welcomed by the next grouse to visit this cover.

Change Was in The Air!

The glorious days of fall are gone as we turn into an immense hollow under a gray, sodden November sky. The leaves are down and the trees look naked. The mountains have a grayish brown color to them. As we grind deeper and deeper into the hollow we begin to gain some altitude.

The old logging road that started low next to the brook trout stream is now skirting the side of the mountain. Immediately we notice something different. The cover has taken on a different tint. Mixed in with the grays, blacks and browns there is a band of blue wild grapes, or fox grapes as the natives call them, hanging in nature's vineyard waiting for all wildlife.

Jan comments on the grapes with a tone of excitement in his voice. He has hunted here long enough to know that grapes mean grouse. The first hard freeze comes in mid November and that brings down the grapes. For the next several weeks, and on into the dead of winter, excellent hunting and dog work will be had under the grape tangles. The vines grow in old tree tops, fallen trees and along the ground around logs. The cover is relatively open and the birds will hold well in the dense cover afforded by the tangles. As Jan stuffed two 16's into his Winchester 21 skeet gun I commented on the bunches of grapes on the ground.

Pixie and Tomba are whining in their crates as they sense our excitement. We would hunt them both as we enjoy seeing a brace of good dogs work grouse. This is steep, rocky country and the footing is tough. Jan would follow the remains of the old tram road as I dropped over the bank to the first flat, or bench as we call them here in Appalachia. The ground was frozen and covered with pods of grapes. I remember thinking I should have brought a plastic bag as they make the best jelly you have ever tasted.

I was brought back to the business at hand by a soft whistle from Jan. He was pointing straight ahead at the same time I realized there were no bells jingling around the mountain. Moving ahead about 50 yards I saw Pixie on point. Another two steps showed that she was backing Tomba who was on point about 20 yards ahead of her.

He was locked onto an immense tangle that grew around an old chestnut snag. Jan was circling to put the tree between him and the dogs. I knew that if either of us went in without circling the tree the grouse would go out the other side undetected. The forest floor was damp and quiet and it appeared that Jan was walking on egg shells. He was in position now and a deep silence fell over the dark woods. I could almost see his white knuckles shining as he gripped the 21 tighter and tighter.

He was like a banjo string as he anticipated the flush. I moved in but nothing happened. I took a couple more steps but still noting. Tomba never moved. He was still as tight and high as when I first saw him. He's in there, I remembered thinking as I took another step. I was in front of the dog now and began to look into the tangle to see if I could spot the grouse. As I bent to peer into the tangle I heard that peeping sound all grouse hunters recognize, made by a grouse when he is startled and feels trapped.

I saw him at about the same time he went into the air. If you have hunted grouse long enough you have heard them start and wondered where they were. It seemed like five seconds before he cleared the tangle and began to hook around the mountain. Jan rushed the first shot and I saw the wad go two feet under the bird. He kept swinging with the 21 and when the grouse was out there about 35 yards he overtook him with a load of 8's. The grouse cartwheeled indicating a broken wing. There was no need to yell fetch, dead bird, or anything else as both dogs were searching for the bird a second after he came down.

I saw Pixie swing past a log and snap into a point. In a second her head dropped and she made a dash ahead about two feet. When she backed out she had a very live grouse in her mouth. Every bird goes to her master and here she came, holding the fluttering grouse by the head only. I quickly dispatched the bird and held it out for Jan and Tomba to admire. It was one of the deep chocolate colored grouse so common to this area. His crop was stuffed with wild grapes. Feathers smoothed Jan gingerly tucked him into his game bag. The beginning of another great day in Nature's Bounty and it was off again, on around the mountain.

Change Was In The Air!

Winter comes hard and stays long in the high Appalachians. With it comes snow and some excellent grouse hunting for those who will brave the elements. We were driving along an old logging road over in Preston County, up tight against the Pennsylvania border. Hemlock, rock walls, apple trees and greenbrier tangles dot this country and make up some of the finest habitat in the Southeastern range of the ruffed grouse. This is the country so beautifully described, and dearly loved, by George Bird Evans. I almost expect to see him coming down the road, following a beautiful pair of orange belton setters at every turn.

Rick Haldeman with a grouse taken from cover too thin to hold grouse, but no one took time to tell the birds. After the winter starts to fade, and we see the warm days of February, grouse will often move back into cover usually reserved for rabbits.

We stopped by an old, fallen, weathered barn surrounded by a smattering of ancient, twisted apple trees. Just below there is a small brook rushing to the Big Sandy. Along the stream are rocks and brush encased in greenbrier vines and its hard, shiny, deep blue-purple berries. When the heavy snows cover the soft mast the grouse will move to the greenbrier for both food and cover. It is a tough fox or hawk indeed that can penetrate the greenbrier to snatch out Old Drummer.

We would hunt Rick's Gunner and my old setter Ginny today. Quite a contrast his snow white, great-grandson of Grouse Ridge Will and my little dark bitch that goes back to Jet Train. Two great grouse dog blood lines that have proven themselves whereever Old Drummer is pursued with pointing dogs. Dropping two 1 oz. loads of 7 1/2's into the 20 gauge 21, I sent Ginny into the creek bottom.

We had worked most of the creek with no sign of a bird. The creek was emptying out into a small clearing, and it was dotted with thornapple trees now barren of their fruit. The haws had long ago been eaten, rotted or covered with the winter's white blanket. But the trees formed the perfect climbing lattice for the greenbrier. The berries were heavy, dark and shiny in the early winter sun. The dogs got to the clearing first and Rick came around a tangle of greenbrier to find Gunner on point. The white dog was hard to see in the bright sun and snow and Rick almost bumped into him before he saw him.

Ginny was coming from the other side and would not see the white dog until it was too late. A soft "whoa" brought her to a stop as she searched for the pointing dog she knew was there somewhere. We had the grouse surrounded as Rick moved closer to Gunner. He would take the shot unless the bird came towards me. I heard the bird start out at the same time I heard Rick yell "coming at you." I was already mounting the 21 when I saw the bird. He saw me at the same time and banked to my right and away from Rick. It was an easy shot and I centered him with the right Skeet 1 barrel just as you would break the low house bird from station three. Ginny saw the bird as it hit with a puff of snow. There is something special about a late winter grouse. I always have a sense of excitement and joy over bagging such a great game bird. On the other hand I have a little sense of remorse about taking one in late winter. I can't help but feel that this great bird almost made it through another winter and would again be looking forward to THE FRUITS OF FALL.

Mount Storm

The Wind, there is always the Wind!

I remember my first trip to Mount Storm as if were yesterday, even though it was 36 years ago. I was in high school and four of us buddies went up to Mount Storm to hunt deer with our friend Bobby Reed. Bobby's dad belonged to the Allegheny Club that hung right on the edge of the Allegheny Front, where the mountain broke over and started its long descent to Petersburg. That club is still there, and the offspring of Bobby and his brother, as well as other members from my home town, still hunt there. It was one of my first real trips into the mountains.

When I walked through the door of their old cabin something caught my eye and it has stuck with me through all these years. Hung neatly, in a line on the wall was a row of leather face masks. As I picture them today, they looked just like what "Jason" wore in his movies. I had to know what they were for. When I asked Bobby, he kind of smiled and said they used them when the wind blew more than normal. He went on to explain that it always blew but sometimes much harder than other times. I thought he was pulling my leg, until we went to bed that is.

About midnight, something was trying to rip the metal roof off the cabin. I sat up and then realized it was the wind. There was a roar over the roof which sounded like it was trying to pull off the sheets of metal roofing. The others woke up and sat there in the darkness talking until Bobby said to go back to sleep, it was just the wind! The next morning it was about 20 degrees and the wind was howling. After only 30 minutes outside we all made a dash for the cabin to get one of the masks. Without one, I am sure our faces would have frozen. The wind never seems to let up on top of the big Allegheny. Like Dolly Sods, it is a world of its own and it creates its own weather.

All of this was going through my head as I rode along Cheat River and started up Cheat Mountain. I thought of the rock there along the road where old John Minico had his wreck when he was first starting to drive. It was a miracle that someone wasn't killed. Tubby Julian got banged up some, as did John Junior when the old man ran smack into the rock cliff at the base of the mountain. I was starting up now and the wind was blowing. I planned to hunt at the edge of Mount Storm, right where it drops off into the big, rugged valley of the North Branch of the Potomac.

I have grouse hunted there now for many years and this is my favorite spot to be at the end of October and up until the middle of November. Tinker, our young Elhew pointer, and Ginny, our nine year old setter, were pawing at their box as I parked and walked to the back of the truck. They know when we have arrived at the chosen spot even though they can't always see it. I had decided to hunt them separately as I didn't want the young dog to depend on the old one to find all the birds while the young one comes along to back each point. If you notice the same dog doing all the backing, you better watch carefully as you probably have a true trailer on your hands.

I was hunting both grouse and woodcock this day in excellent cover for grouse and for migrating woodcock on their way south. While I was slipping bells and orange collars on the dogs and stuffing a few 20 gauge shells into my vest pocket, I noticed that the wind had died down a little. Even though it always blows, there are quiet pockets tucked into the hollows deep between those small ridges on top of the mountain.

I remember thinking that it might even be a pretty nice day for a change. I pointed Tinker into the covert, pulled my hat on tighter, and followed along. She was working beautifully. First one side and then the other, but always going to the cover, the birdy looking objectives. No need to quarter in front of me, as the cover was on both sides of the little hollow I was following into the valley where the beaver dams were. I hoped a few woodcock had decided to stay and wait out the storm that had swept into the area a day ago.

We had hunted about an hour and not moved a single bird of any kind. I was starting to wonder if the cold, light rain and the wind that was starting to kick up now was affecting the birds. I have hunted through a cover in the rain and never moved a single grouse. Later in the afternoon, after the sun had popped out and dried things up, I have walked the same covert and moved a grouse in every likely looking spot.

Grouse will get under logs and brush piles in a rain and not move at all. After they sit there motionless for a while the scent seems to hold very close to their bodies, and unless the dog practically steps on them, he can't seem to wind them.

The rain was coming harder now in long, gray sheets. I was already soaked so no need to turn back now. The only good thing was the temperature. It was in the high 50's and as long as we kept moving I didn't really notice the cold. As we started on around the valley, where the beaver ponds were, Tinker went into a large tangle of greenbrier that was laced through an old hawthorn tree. This was near a few autumn olive trees that were loaded with fruit. Autumn olive seemed to be the only thing that really hit in the area this year and the grouse, turkey and even the bears were feeding heavily on them. There were several trees scattered around where the bears had ridden down and broken the limbs to get at the berries.

Tinker went into the clump of cover and her bell went dead silent. Peering into the cover I could see her pointing intently into the center of the tangle near the base of the tree. I made a quick circle to the right trying to put the bird between the dog and me. Mister grouse must have been watching me. He decided not to wait until I got into position and exploded out of the tangle. That was his mistake.

Instead of going away or to the left he hooked back to the right and began to reach for altitude. The little Belgian Browning 20 gauge over and under was already on the way to my shoulder when he went up. Behind a bush he went but I kept the gun swinging and picked him up when he came out of the other side. It was a long shot but as the barrels passed his nose I slapped the trigger. Centered with an ounce of hard 8's the bird folded in mid air, crashing through a small bush and onto the damp forest floor. Tinker was on him immediately and soon came to me with head held high and proud. A perfect piece of dog work.

After a few pictures of a proud, young pointer and her grouse, the bird was carefully tucked into the game bag. It seems disrespectful to simply cram a bird into your bag to later emerge as a mangled ball of twisted, broken feathers. A game bird is one of the few creatures that has beauty in both life and death. We headed on around the valley and started the long climb back up to the top where the truck was parked. The wind was gusting harder now and the sky was black and ominous. The clouds seemed to be racing across the sky at tree top level. I was watching out ahead as we continued through this section of big, mature timber. I didn't really expect to find any birds here but it was the shortest way back to the truck. I planned to put Tinker up and take Ginny to another piece of cover for the afternoon hunt.

We were in the middle of the big woods when I heard the train coming. Problem was, there are no tracks up here. The nearest train tracks are over in Gormania several miles away. I stopped to locate the source of the noise. Tinker heard it too and was right at my side, up tight against my left leg. Then we heard it. A loud snap and then another and another, all the time coming closer and closer. The train was coming and it was snapping the tops out of the big, old dead trees as it roared across the Allegheny Front.

At that very moment the ghost of an old man came back across my mind. I hadn't seen him in over 35 years and hadn't given him a thought for at least six or seven. When I worked at The Sport Store, some 35 years ago, there was an old man who came in about three or four times a week. He didn't talk much, just stood in the corner listening and sucking on his pipe that he also used to call turkeys. He was tall and thin with sharp, distinct features, wire rimmed glasses and a Brier pipe glued between his front teeth. All I ever knew him by was Old Man Findley.

I never forgot him for two reasons. The first was that he owned a perfect Winchester Model 70, .270 Super Grade. When he got too old to hunt he sold it to Leo, the owner of the store and I lost track of it. Back then money was scarce so it didn't really make any difference where it went, I couldn't have afforded it anyway.

But today I remembered him for something he said. He didn't talk much but sometimes when only the two of us were in the store he would tell me of his early hunting adventures. He hunted before seasons were established. Back then their seasons to hunt were governed by the weather. They started when they figured the nights were cold enough to chill the meat and start the drying process for the long winter.

He used to talk of their trips into Pocahontas and Randolph Counties. They would take horses, wagons and big wall tents with stoves and stay in the mountains for two or three weeks hunting whatever they could find. At that moment I remembered him saying, "if you are in the mountains, when The Train is coming, and the timber starts to cracking, get out and get out quick!"

There was no time to dwell upon the meaning and I didn't have to tell Tinker to heel. She was stuck to my heels as I made a run for it as fast as I could leave that big timber. I unloaded my gun and took off like a broken field half back. I was dodging between tree trunks, stepping from rock to rock, jumping over fallen timber and all the while looking back over my shoulder at he tops of the trees that were snapping behind me. In a lot less time than it took us to get into the covert we were out.

We headed back out into the valley and the fields where the beaver ponds were located. There were limbs and branches falling all around us and I expected any moment to get smacked with one. The Big Man was watching out for old Frank and Tinker this day and we made it out of the timber with no problem. That was the hardest blowing storm I have ever encountered in the mountains while hunting anywhere. Later in the afternoon we heard on the radio that the weather service's tracking station over by the New Stoney River Dam clocked the gusts at 65 miles per hour!

Safe and sound in the pickup we rode out the storm while I sipped hot coffee. Tinker was on the floor of the front seat while she dried out before returning to her kennel box in the back. I don't know where all the water went, but as it went by us it was parallel with the ground and headed for Old

Stony River Dam. The main brunt of the storm seemed to have passed by now and, although the wind was still blowing, it didn't seem dangerous. Any sane person would have headed for home. Did anyone ever say that bird hunters were sane? Not that I am aware of.

Like any true bird hunter I decided to give Ginny her chance in the covert, even if only for an hour or less. She had waited patiently in her box and I was not about to disappoint her. I have hauled her all day when some circumstance prevented her from getting her turn and it bothered me almost as much as it did her. We headed on out working our way across the covert to the other side where a little valley winds its way over the edge and heads to Elk Garden. It is damp here and always a good place for woodcock.

An early storm had dumped six inches of snow but it was gone and I hoped some of the woodcock had ridden out the storm and remained. If the Good Lord ever created a better working and handling dog, and one that was more of a pleasure to hunt with than Ginny, he must have kept it for himself. Ginny was cutting up the cover in her naturally snappy, efficient manner as I leisurely walked behind enjoying the picture unfolding before me.

I have never followed a happier dog, one that enjoyed what she was doing more than this little black setter. John Stewart had bred and raised her litter and sold her to me when she was about 14 months old. She was almost all black and her color kept her from being picked when her litter mates went to different hunters across Pennsylvania.

She showed her potential when we took her to Manitoba in 1987 where she made 14 productive points in a couple of hours the first afternoon we had her on the ground. It was amazing how much whiter she became from that day on. She covers every likely looking spot while hunting at a speed at which most dogs chase cats. The amazing thing about her ground coverage is that she is everywhere, in front, back, to the sides, up and down but never really out of contact. She knows where we are at all times and continually checks to see if we are all on the same page as she slices through the cover.

She dropped into the little run, hit the other bank hard, came out and when she topped the far bank slammed into a low intense point. From her intensity and low stance I knew she came up out of the creek and smack into a bird on the bank. I had to drop down and cross the little ditch in order to get into shooting position. Grabbing a small whip of a sapling I pulled myself to the top of the bank. Just as my feet got under me the woodcock went out. It was a typical towering flush and leaning back some I lost my balance a little. I had my left foot behind me when I shot and knew that the

Browning was under the towering bird. Maple shavings were still in the air when I regained my balance and took that split second to get my foot forward and the barrels on the bird.

Just as the barrels caught up to the woodcock I pulled the trigger and the modified barrel did its job. The bird was dead in the air, and with feathers drifting on the breeze, pitched into the tall grass. There is no command to fetch as this old matriarch knows the drill very well. In a moment she was sitting in front of me with a very large woodcock draping out of either side of her mouth. I am always awed by the softness, the gentleness and the warm, soft colors of the woodcock, true class in ever respect.

With the woodcock tucked neatly into the game bag, we were off again. We were working our way back toward the truck when we came to a little glade that was choked with hazel brush. The hazel rimmed little clearings of bare ground except for areas covered with strawberry leaves and teaberry. A few scattered pines were sprinkled through the covert. The little island of cover was completely surrounded by a dark bog thick with tag alder.

As Ginny started to circle the little clearings I could almost smell woodcock myself. Ginny darted in and out of the tag alder, and tracking her movement by the sound of her bell I suddenly realized she had stopped. A soft whistle brought no response, telling me that she was stacked up on a bird. If she just stopped to listen for me, she would resume her movement; if she's on point, all the whistling or yelling will not get her to move.

I started to make my way to her through the maze of alder trunks. Bent over, snaking my way into the wet area I saw Ginny ahead about 40 yards. I swung to the right to put myself in front of her for the final approach. If I could get past that fallen tree I would be in good position for a shot. Just as I ducked to go under the tree the woodcock sprang into the air not fifteen feet from my face.

I lunged forward to clear the tree and came up swinging. The bird went up through the tag alder and then hooked back to the left over the dog. Just as I thought he was gone, he crossed a sunlit opening in the canopy. The barrels were still tracking his movement and I hit the trigger the instant they covered him. The load of 8's shredded the leaves around the bird and broke a wing. Ginny was tracking his flight also and had him when he hit the ground. Another large female was added to the game bag. A brace of woodcock added to the grouse we already had made for a special bag.

We had enjoyed the moment with the first one. After the second one, the wind picked up and I could see dark clouds across the Allegheny Front again. I even thought I heard The Train coming. Ginny had her turn and I had a great day. We had beaten Mount Storm once today, and to do it again might be too much to expect. We left, but knew that when we do return there will be the wind, always the wind.

Grouse in the Mountain Vineyards

When the grapes hit in Appalachia you must abandon your traditional, upland coverts and plunge deep into the dark abysses on Mother Nature's Mountain Vineyards.

As I stood looking up into the treetops, which were bent from the weight of a heavy crop of dark, blue-purple wild grapes, I couldn't help but recall the ancient fable of The Old Fox. These grapes of the mountain vineyards, hopelessly out of his reach, were surely the sour grapes he turned his pointed nose up at and walked away from. While they remain sour and out of reach of all ground dwellers, the two ruffed grouse, who had just left a limb bouncing with their departure, found them very much to their liking.

Neither Tomba nor I had a fair chance at those two grouse as we walked along working the thick tangles of grape vines that choked the tree trunks of the flat we were on. Tomba had pointed earlier and I flushed a single grouse from in front of the point. That bird had been buried deep in a jumble of vines and logs the size of a small pickup truck. It was obvious that the grouse had found the grapes and were gorging themselves on those that still hung in the trees as well as those that Jack Frost and the mountain winds had put on the ground.

We were working along an old haul road at the base of a strip-mine highwall. To my right, the sheer highwall rose up some 60 feet or so. At the top was a narrow bench covered with 10 to 15 foot high timber that was strangled with greenbrier. To the left there was a 25 foot strip of brush, laced with wild grapes before the ground fell away sharply 40 feet to the next bench that was crisscrossed with rotting, old logs that were crawling with the twisted, gnarled grapevines.

Tomba was working the strip on the left, weaving back and forth from the lip of the bank to the middle of the road I was following. The dirt and rocks had been shoved up on the right to form a sort of dike. I was watching Tomba float silently along, like a cloud of blue and white smoke, except for the lonely tinkle of the tiny sleigh bell.

I was moving in a daydream, engulfed in the sounds of the wind through the timber, the roar of the river far below and the soft tinkle of the bell. This was mountain cover comprised of maple, oak, scattered pine and clumps of bright, green laurel. Add to this the blue of the grapes and the gray and black of the fallen wet grape leaves and you had an ever changing kaleidoscope of color.

I was relaxed, moving effortlessly along the old haul road that snaked its way around the mountain. With the overhanging grapevines I had the feeling of walking through a high, shaded tunnel. For a moment I seemed lost, wandering aimlessly through nature's wine cellar. So heavy were the grapes this year that their aroma hung in the mountain air currents. I found myself stopped, staring for a moment at the statue-like figure of Tomba ahead of me with his long-feathered high tail before I was brought back to the mountain and the moment at hand.

Tomba had his head, and half his body, stuck into the waist high grass at the edge of the old road. Ten feet in front of his stare the bank dropped away 40 feet to the flat below. I followed his glassy gaze, but it seemed he was staring out into space. I walked out in front of him but no grouse flushed. "Tomba", I said, "did your bird escape undetected?" His gaze never faltered. The wind was hard in his face, and he appeared to get taller as he stood there on his tiptoes. The ground was bare at the edge of the bank, and there was no place for a grouse to hide. Walking back to Tomba's side I again followed his eyes out over the mountain and into the trees ahead. There, about 20 feet in front of him and 20 feet up in a tree sat a big cock grouse surrounded by large clumps of wild grapes.

When our eyes met, the bird appeared to simply fall forward, like a small dive bomber. I was mounting the 20 gauge, Winchester 21 as he fell. I knew I had to get underneath his path, and just as I passed him I pulled the trigger. At the same moment the grouse opened his wings, flared his tail, banked and sailed away to the left. My shot went right through the hole he left with his zigzag flight. Before I could recover he dropped over the lip of the mountain and out of sight.

One moment a blinding flash of feathers and the thunder of a shot, and the next calm and silence. I explained to Tomba what a great grouse dog he was, which he accepted very graciously with a sparkle in those big, dark, soft eyes, and we were off around the mountain again.

We left the cool shade of a deep hollow shaded with hanging vines, rounded a sunny, laurel covered point, and plunged right back into another rock studded, dank, dark crevice of a valley where the forest floor was splotched with a soft shade of blue from fallen grapes. Tomba passed me and headed uphill. I followed, picking my way over and around the rocks, logs, briers and tangles of grapevines.

Old logging roads crisscross all of Appalachia. Here, Tomba has a grouse pinned just over the bank as John Jezioro circles to pin the bird between the gun and the dog.

Reaching the limit of his uphill cast Tomba swapped ends and started back down. As he moved near an old dead snag cloaked with grapes, it appeared that he ran into an obstacle so hard that his front end lowered and his back end jacked up into the air. The invisible wall was the sweet scent of grouse.

I dropped down a few yards, hooked back to the right and came at the dog from his left front. There was no movement except the rolling of Tomba's eyes as he heard me approaching. I was thinking that if I could clear that log over there to the right, by that heart shaped rock draped in dark green moss, I would be in good position for a shot. Tomba was locked onto the tangle 15 feet in front of him, and there was no doubt the grouse was in there.

I had one foot over the log, and the other was about to touch the ground when out they came. The first came out and shot down the mountain. I stumbled a little but regained control as the barrels overtook the bird. I was off balance but the shot was good, and the grouse went into a tail over teacup tumble, with its momentum taking it out over the lip of the mountain.

At the shot, Tomba was streaking downhill after the cartwheeling bird, when at the same instant two more birds burst from the tangle. The one on the left disappeared in a low, curling flight around the point of the mountain. The one on the right went uphill and made a semicircle which brought it back, high over my head. I remembered to get well ahead of the grouse before mashing the trigger. At the shot the bird seemed to deflate and completely collapse, with his head and neck falling limp indicating a head or neck shot.

I marked his falling path by the shower of leaves and small twigs as well as the solid thud when he hit the ground. I was making my way to the second bird when Tomba proudly delivered his bird to my hand. With two plump grouse in the bag we took a break to admire their colors and examine their bulging crops. As expected both were stuffed to the hilt with the wild grapes, a few pieces of clover and some other green leaves that I couldn't identify.

This hunt was an echo of many I have had over the past 30 years all through the coverts of Appalachia. Many hunters unfamiliar with the country where wild grapes grow often overlook an opportunity to experience this great hunting because they fail to recognize it as grouse cover.

We all know that grouse like young growth, scrub timber that is studded with shrubs. We all know that the birds like the edges of old abandoned pasture fields that are coming back in hawthorn. Everything you read talks about hunting the edges. Hunt the edges of big timber, the edges of old fields and the edges of the old logging roads that dissect the range of the ruffed grouse. When in the Lake States, you search out the clear cuts where 15 foot aspen is mixed in with pine and a little mature timber.

All this advice is sound. These are the classic upland coverts that we all like to hunt. But there comes a time when you must plunge into the old age forest where Mother Nature has strung thousands of miles of twisting, climbing, clinging grapevines. It takes a few years for the vines to bear and they usually occur around the bigger, older timber. They seem to do best in the damp, shaded recesses of the deep hollows where the soil may be rocky, but rich.

When the grapes hit, they offer both food and cover to the birds for an extended period of time. The grapes will hang in the trees until several hard frosts and the winds knock them to the ground. In most of Appalachia, the grouse will move into the grapes in early November. They will sit in the trees and feed as well as scratch the leaves for those grapes that have fallen. When the first heavy snows come, the birds will often stay in the grapes for the protection the tangles provide. I have had more multiple flushes, two to ten birds, while hunting the grape coverts than any other.

You will also have some of your best dog work under the canopy of the grapes. The shade of the bigger timber, and the vines, keeps out the sun and discourages a lot of thick grass and smaller brush. This presents a relatively open covert, except for the clumps that surround the trunks of the trees, or piles of logs, or that choke and cling to old dead snags and timbered treetops. This also creates a damp condition where scent seems to flow unrestricted.

One of my most vivid memories of dogs on point came in mature, old timber draped with ancient grapevines from the size of my thumb to the size of my forearm. So heavy was the canopy above us that it almost seemed we were hunting in the shade of a tent. I was hunting Tomba, our English setter and Pixie, our Elhew pointer. Long slivers of light splashed down on the forest floor with intermittent blankets of sun creeping into the darkness every time a cloud moved.

We were high on a vertical mountainside above the North Branch of the Potomac. The canyon was so steep and deep that there was very little sun that reached the ground except when the sun was at its apex. Because of this there was very little ground cover. The two white dogs were a stark contrast in this world of dark shadows. They were like noiseless ghosts as they floated in and out of the dark tree trunks.

We were on one of the little benches, and out ahead of me about 50 yards there was a mass of vines smothering an old fallen tree. I watched as the dogs approached the tangle from different sides. Tomba went in behind it first and disappeared. I was watching Pixie close on the treetop when I saw her gait change to that of a cat on broken glass. She was still 15 yards from the jumble when she stopped in a low, intense back. It was obvious that she was backing Tomba who was on point behind the screen of limbs and vines.

I circled to the right and came around the trunk of the tree. There, 20 yards ahead of me was Tomba, standing high on both ends, as if electrified by some unseen force. At that exact moment the clouds moved to let long, snaky fingers of sunlight dance across the dogs. They almost seemed to be flashing as the sun rolled over them. Mesmerized by the sight of two such great grouse dogs I stood glued to he ground. Only the single tinkle of Pixie's bell as she tired and put her raised foot on the ground, brought me back.

I would like to tell you that I walked in and took that grouse out of the air with one good shot but it didn't happen. I took a step toward Tomba and the bird came out, hooked to he left and went low over Pixie preventing my shot. As soon as he cleared Pixie he dropped over the lip of the mountain and out of sight. That we didn't take that bird was of little significance. The sight of those two white dogs growing out of that dark forest floor, with splotches of sunlight dancing across their backs, will be in my mind's eye for as long as the Good Lord lets me recall the glorious moments I have enjoyed chasing old ruff through the Mountain Vineyards of Appalachia.

CHAPTER 5

WINTER; IT'S NOT LIKE HUNTING THE GLORIOUS DAYS OF FALL

It was the first of February and the snow ran deep, high above the Cheat River. Tom Stalnaker had been in the area last fall for an afternoon's turkey hunting and noted moving four or five grouse while walking the old logging roads. We were loading the dogs when my neighbor stopped. He commented that with the 20 degree temperature, and the -5 degree wind chill, the grouse might not be out moving and feeding. He was right, but like I told him, they had to be somewhere!

The 4X4 groaned, spun, dug and bounced along, ever up, until we were on the high plateau that looks out over the Cheat River and Preston County. Like much of this country it had been strip mined 15 or 20 years ago. As part of the reclamation program they had planted it heavy with autumn olive. The higher ridges and deep hollows were still cloaked in their native greenbrier and wild grape cover.

Bells on the setter Tomba, and the Elhew pointer Pixie, we started off down through some thick autumn olive cover. There were six to eight inches of snow on the ground and we could see that all the ground cover had been flattened by the heavy snow, leaving none for a grouse to hide. We decided to go to a high ridge on the other side of the stripped area. We could see, even from this distance, that the ridge was laced with grape vines and greenbrier. As soon as we got deeper into the heavy cover, we saw grouse tracks that appeared to be at least one or two days old. With the bright sun, even though the temperature hovered at 20 degrees, we were surprised that we weren't finding a fresh track or two. We knew from the tracks the birds were still in the area, but it was clear they were not out feeding.

Many of the mountain tops in this part of the country are covered with boulders that were pushed to the surface thousands of years ago. Soon we found ourselves standing in the middle of room sized boulders with no safe way through. Nothing to do but backtrack and look for a way around. Dropping down a little we got out of the boulders and were able to again travel the ridge. The cover was near perfect for late season hunting. The rocks, slashings, old tree tops and logs were hooked together with greenbrier and grape vines. Grouse could move through this tangle in safety and have both food and cover close at hand.

From my experience, grouse don't like to move great distance when the ground is covered with snow. I think they realize they are easily spotted by predators as they move across open snow. The birds seem to know this is an especially dangerous time as hawks can sit in trees, undetected high above the forest floor, and swoop down on unsuspecting prey. Their reluctance to leave heavy cover was clearly demonstrated later in the day.

Once we got around the rocks we found ourselves on the back of the mountain with the Cheat glimmering far below like a shimmering ribbon in the wind as the water and ice clashed. The wind was up now and we couldn't hear the bells of the dogs. Walking to the very edge of the mountain, Tom spotted Tomba at once. With a soft whistle he got my attention and I started moving toward him and the dogs. Tom was in position now and I was moving around for the flush. Before I could get to the dog, a grouse shot out from under the tree top. Just as Tom cut loose with his 20 gauge double the bird hooked sharply to the left. A quick second shot passed closer to the mark but still only resulted in another salute to the quickly departing bird.

Tomba was still standing there, and before Tom could reload, or before I could move to the edge for a better view, another grouse roared off over the side of the mountain keeping low and out of sight. The young setter broke and chased the bird for a few yards while Tom and I stood there with a little grouse egg on our faces. As we stood there Pixie, the pointer, came swinging by to look for the dead bird she was sure was there. After all, she had heard the shooting. As she swung up wind of the tangle she wheeled and pointed into the logs. I told Tom there was a lot of scent there from the two grouse that had just flown out. Before she got there I had kicked the tree just to make sure another late riser wasn't sulking below. We were standing there with guns at our sides waiting for Pixie to move on as the scent dissipated. You guessed it. The scent didn't dissipate, it got stronger, the dog got staunch and just as I started to tell Tom that there might be another one in there, it left. Three birds and nary a feather! But that's why they call it grouse hunting instead of grouse shooting.

With three birds behind us on the ridge there was nothing to do but make a short cast back to see if one might be relocated. We split the ridge, Tom on one side of the boulders and me on the other. We were working into the wind and my eyes were watering pretty bad. I had to drop below the crest to get through the thick understory. About the time I was below the ridge I heard Tom yell, "point!" He knew to move in and wait if the bird held until I got there. If the bird didn't wait he would be in position. The grouse had hit the ground and then run into a grape tangle at the base of a tree. Tom was ready this time, and when the bird started out he caught up with it with the right barrel and a one ounce load of 7 1/2's.

That one in the bag we continued on our original course, which brought us to a big pine plantation. The trees were thirty feet high and thick. We had to go through them to get to the other cover we wanted to hunt. "I heard one go out," Tom yelled fifty yards to my left. He came out of a tree directly over him and went on out ahead of us.

We continued on as the dogs searched the cover under the pines. "There he goes again," Tom yelled out as I heard the faint thunder of the wings. Straight out ahead of us again, and again out of a tree. We hoped that he would hit the ground this time but knew that grouse usually fly into the same type cover they first flushed from. We were nearing the end of the pines now and the cover opened up into a nice thicket. I thought we might have him now if he had gone into the thicket. Just as we were about 20 feet from the end of the pines the bird again flushed from overhead and went tearing right back over our heads where he had first come from. This wise, old bird knew exactly where he was going. I hope he passes those crafty old genes on to the next generation.

As we were near a likely-looking spot in the thicket, the dogs swung across in front of us and locked up on what we called a divide find. If the bird held, there would be no escape without a fair chance at him. Tom was on the right and I made a quick half circle to the left. The dogs were between us and locked onto a clump of greenbrier that encased an old snag. The forest got quiet as we waited for the flush. When nothing happened after about 15 seconds I took a step. That's all it took. The bird came out hard on Tom's side and went straight up the high wall to his right. Tom is a vary fast gun and had two shots off before the bird reached the top. The second wasn't necessary but he couldn't stop even after he saw the first connect. The bird came down just on top of the highwall edge. Pixie was the first to the top of the bank and scooped up the flopping bird in one quick, swift motion. She quickly delivered a still alive bird to my hand.

I dispatched the bird and took a moment to admire the deep chestnut, reddish brown colors. While I appreciate the beauty of all grouse, I still think our birds of Appalachia are the most beautiful to be found anywhere. The gray ones of the Lake States have a beauty of their own but it is the red ones that spell splendor and class.

There were no tracks visible where the bird came out, so we went over to check. Sure enough, there was a roost with several droppings in it and not a fresh track. Since it had snowed the day before, we felt the bird had sat there, without venturing out, for at least a day. The only track was the two or three where he had come out from the shelter of the log before roaring off into the frozen blue sky. We wondered how many grouse had waited us out on this day as we passed by. It was clear that if the dogs didn't pass close enough to wind the tight-sitting bird, it would not move. After a bird has sat motionless for a period of time I am convinced the "cloud of scent " that engulfs it is extremely small. When they are sitting there with feathers drawn in tight I don't think much scent escapes. That's why we seem to have much better dog work when we find feeding birds in the late afternoon.

With two fine grouse in the bag, and the wind kicking up to 20 and 25 M.P.H. it was time to leave this high mountain cover and seek the shelter of the valleys below. Not easy, this late winter hunting, and not for everyone. But to the dyed-in-the-wool grouse hunter, there is beauty in the cold and the bleakness of winter. The blanket of snow covers the thickets with a silence. The little sleigh bells around the necks of our pointing dogs seem right at home in this winter wonderland. And besides, it beats the hell out of Saturday afternoon football!

When the Snow Falls, Hunt the Roses

When I topped Cheat Mountain and started out across that high plateau that runs to The Allegheny Front, the dogs and I became part of a Christmas card setting. We were now in a winter wonderland. Ice and snow hung heavy on the branches and the trees appeared to be dressed in large tufts of soft, fluffy cotton. Limbs the size of pencils were now the size of my fingers. Barbed wire fences along the road were now a half inch in diameter as they sat encased in a crystal cocoon. Winter had come early to the Allegheny Highlands and was hanging on as we headed on east towards mount Storm.

One of the country's most dedicated grouse biologists, West Virginia's Tom Allen, ages a grouse as prepares to fit it with a tiny radio transmitter as part of an extensive study in Appalachia.

Our grouse hunting had been shut down for nearly a month during deer and bear season. I hunt both deer and bear, and part of the reason is that I often find good grouse habitat or make new contacts.

This year, I had been accepted by a group of the local bear hunters and was allowed to follow along during the last hunts of the season. I was referred to as the writer who hunted grouse with his bird dogs. In addition to a great outreach of friendship, I was being given invaluable information on where I might look for grouse. No one covers the country like those who live there and roam it every month of the year either hunting or scouting. These were men who knew their country and their game. They began to look for grouse and grouse cover and let me know where it was.

Dick Heavner was the Hunt Master, and with Scott, Mike, Shawn, Allen and Larry taking note of grouse flushed, I soon had more grouse country than I could hunt that year. Scott had taken me into a steep hillside laced with a thick covering of multiflora rose. The hillside hooked to the right and ended in a vast hollow shrouded with room size clumps of rose bushes so dense that not even a fox could get into the birds that roosted there.

When the snow falls, and hangs on for a week or more, the grouse will often forsake their grapevine cover and fly out into these old mountain fields and hollows. The Dept. of Agriculture classified the wild roses as a noxious weed and has done everything it could to eradicate them from Appalachia. But like the tough mountaineers who inhabit this country, the wild roses flourish. They may be the most important plant we have for winter survival of all birds, game and non game alike. The sharp, hooked thorns will turn away any and all predators. Grouse and rabbits can sit in the middle of these tangles and be safe from predators of the sky and ground. The real benefit comes in the food the wild roses furnish. During these harsh winter conditions, the grouse can sit in and under the roses and both feed and roost. They don't have to travel from feeding to roosting area and can conserve energy as well as having a good, open view of the predators.

I was high above the North Branch now and had to stop for a moment to thank the Big Man. How fortunate we are and how much we take for granted. The sun was trying to peek from breaks in the snow clouds, and bits and pieces of bright blue danced across the highlands as the clouds parted and regrouped. As much as they try even the most talented artists fall short when trying to duplicate what laid before me. There is simply no artist who can capture the magnificence of these mountains we call The Appalachians. Only the Big Man could create such a vista that spread before these humble eyes, and for that I thanked him.

Jan Riffe and Tinker take a moment to admire a winter grouse. When the snows come, hunt the cover with a mixture of shrubs, brush and conifers.

Tomba was whimpering in his box as he sensed we had arrived at the designated place for the days hunt. I think George Bird Evans was the first I read who pointed out that some of the best hunting, and scenting conditions come about after a storm roars across the high country and quiet, sunny days follow. It is during these days of sun when the fluffy snow softens that hunting improves greatly.

Bell and orange collar around his neck, Tomba was cast into the wind. He was cutting the cover from one side to the other as I walked the grown-over road that made its way up and around the mountain. I was below a huge patch of wild roses that were choking an old snag of a walnut tree when they started out. They were above the road and Tomba below, so he had no idea what was going on.

Not more than 20 yards above me grouse were going out one at a time. Their flushes were easy to identify and, as near as I could tell, there were seven different in this group. This is very common late in December, after snow comes, as grouse seem to congregate at these food and cover sources.

As they flushed, I was catching little flashes of feathers each time they passed a hole in the cover. From the glimpses I caught, it appeared they were going around the hill in the direction I was headed. Also it appeared they were staying high and not plunging low below the road I was on. I knew it was a long way out to the hollow beyond, and felt the birds would scatter out on the hillside above the road.

In a minute, Tomba was back beside me and I sent him above the road. He began to search up and down the bank as he worked his way toward the hollow ahead. It was easy to keep track of him by both sight and the sound of his small sleigh bell. He was headed downhill at a dead run when suddenly he drew up into a high, intense point. He was locked onto a small autumn olive bush about 15 feet in front of him. With a fair breeze in his nose the scent was good and he had his grouse nailed. The cover here was fairly open for mountain cover, and I had most of all the escape routes covered as I took my first steps toward the dog.

It is good to hunt with a dog who you know well. When Tomba doesn't move his head at all to see if I am coming, he is sure. He was fixed on the bush and never blinked as I approached. The 20 gauge 21 was stuffed full with 1oz. loads of 8's. I was ready and my heart was pounding from the slight climb up to the dog, but more from the excitement of approaching a dog on point. People ask if I still get excited approaching a point after 35 years of following pointing dogs. The answer, of course, is YES, followed by the comment that if I ever loose that excitement I will hand the 21 and the Browning to my sons and bid the highlands farewell.

I saw a flicker of movement under the bush just as the grouse took a step or two to get far enough out to take wing. The gun was coming to my shoulder while I tracked him with my eyes as he broke free of the cover. He was coming out high now and reaching for altitude when the barrels passed his nose. Just as the gun overtook him I mashed the trigger. The grouse cartwheeled in a shower of soft, brown feathers and plunged into the snow on the road below. Tomba was on him before his last flutter, and I had to chuckle as I watched. The bird was still flopping a little and Tomba now held him down with his front foot while he improved his grip. He brought the bird to me and put the warm, limp bird in my outstretched hand. Tomba loves to retrieve and I always toss the bird out again for him. This done we took a moment to admire the soft, rich, browns of this winter grouse. I think their colors become more vivid as winter progresses.

Carefully tucking the bird into my game pouch, we were off again. Tomba had it figured out now and stayed above the road. He seemed to sense that the grouse were on the sidehill and not below the road in the bigger timber. The hillside cover was about 200 yards wide with a cleared pasture field on top and the little winding road below. Tomba was about 75 yards above me and working on an angle that was bringing him back down to my level.

When he was about 50 yards away I saw him slow, check the wind, and then take two or three steps forward toward a downed log. The old log had long ago fallen to be covered with the wild roses and a flat autumn olive bush. There was even a little bit of greenbrier laced through the tangle. Tomba was nailed to the ground with that expression that says," he's in here, get ready, and don't let him get away with a poor shot!"

Working up toward Tomba, the little 20 gauge 21 was poised in the ready position. I got up to the tangle but nothing happened. Looking again at the dog there was not a bit of doubt in those big, soft, dark eyes. I was looking right at the dog and had the tangle between me and Tomba. I waited a while, thinking the pause would be too much pressure for the grouse. If he was in there, he was sitting tight. Only about 10 feet from the tangle now and I could feel my hands tighten around the straight grip of the gun. Where is he Tomba, I asked out loud as if Tomba could answer. He didn't answer but the grouse did. Like we all know, the human voice will often put a bird in flight. It did this time and I heard him peeping before I heard him take wing. It was thick and he was beating the brush as he fought to free himself from the safety of the overhanging cover.

The gun was half up before the bird cleared the cover and he had only one way to go. Driving straight around the hill he presented a high house number three shot. I swung quickly to cover him before he reached the turn of the hill. Just as the barrels caught up with him I hit the trigger and saw him fold. His momentum carried him on for about 10 yards before he hit the snow. Again Tomba was on him as quickly as he had flushed. What a picture he presented as he came prancing up the hill with his bird. Head high, tail erect he came as proud as I was with the shot. He knew he had done his job well and could sense the pride I had in him. At three years of age he was becoming what we call a GROUSE DOG. That sense of finding grouse and holding them with solid points was coming out in him with each bird he found that year.

The birds were holding well and life was good in the Alleghenies. We went on around the hill that afternoon and Tomba pointed five more grouse. I shot one more and then emptied the gun. There were grouse on the mountain that day and Tomba was picking them apart. With the gun emptied and camera ready, I followed that setter while he showed what he was made of. There was no need to shoot another that day. What would it prove? What does taking a limit mean? There are days when the birds hold, the shooting is open, and the dog nails them to the ground. On those days it is no real feat to take a limit of birds.

And then there are days when you can't buy a shot. Oh, we shoot and shoot again but in reality we never had a true shot. So it is again the Good Lord, in his infinite wisdom, who knows when to let this humble scribe have a great day of success. He knows that it takes a little success now and then to keep us all coming back time and time again into this beautiful country we call the high country. As we left the mountain I stopped to take one last look, and hoped it really wouldn't be!

CHAPTER 6

MINING FOR GROUSE
WEST VIRGINIA'S STRIP MINE GROUSE

There is More Than Black Gold In The Southern Coalfields

After a recent documentary on West Virginia, I had the chance to walk those very mountains so rich in the history and culture of our state. The best way to learn strange country is to go with a native of the area and, while at a sportsman's show in Charleston, I had the good fortune to meet one. To top it off, he was a true grouse hunter. When he invited me to hunt with him for a day, I jumped at the chance.

After a drive of 180 miles I arrived at Jared's home in Peck's Mill. Jared is a fine young man who very early in life has discovered the thrill and joy of bird hunting. Unlike many his age, he doesn't have to have 100 pounds of dead meat at the end of the day to have had a great time. He was ready to go when I arrived and in a few minutes we were heading on south in Logan County. Jared had decided to leave his young setter at home this day to have the opportunity to see another dog work.

After about 30 minutes of winding around and up we came to the top of the mountain. The area is unlike our own part of the state, with its narrow valleys and steep mountains. There are simply no flat spots as we know them. There are no benches on the mountains and the mountains must surely rise at an angle of nearly 60 degrees! We had a lot to share as we drove to the spot. Jared's family were coal miners, as was my grandfather and many of our readers. We could relate to the struggles of the southern coal fields and the harshness of the land.

But we were here to grouse hunt and it was a beautiful day. Warm, sunny and fairly quiet, it promised to be about perfect for such a late season grouse hunt. When we were making our plans over the phone, Jared had asked if I was bringing anyone with me. I answered that I was coming alone but was wondering why he had asked. As we neared the spot where we would park the truck he mentioned that, since I was his guest, I could "walk first." These two statements had me puzzled but I quickly saw the reason for his questions and comments. It wasn't that he didn't want anyone else to hunt with us. It was simply that three people would have a difficult time spreading out enough to hunt. The old grown up strip road we were to follow around the mountain was barely wide enough for two to walk side by side comfortably. In most places we had to walk single file while the dog worked both sides and ahead. This is why "the guest" got to walk first, to take advantage of any shot that might present itself.

We decided to hunt Ginny, our eight year old setter, first. Tomba and Pixie would wait their turn. Around the mountain we went with Ginny working the narrow bench ahead. Pretty soon we saw her locked up looking at the edge where the mountain dropped off into what seemed like eternity. Jared started in from the side as I attempted to get a shot with the camera. He hadn't gone but a few steps when the grouse came out. The bird shot straight out over the edge and immediately dropped out of sight heading for the bottom. I wasn't prepared for the sight that greeted me when I walked to the edge to see where the bird had gone.

There, almost straight down, was a tiny community of fairly new houses set along the banks of a glistening creek. It reminded me of one of the tiny hamlets scattered among the mountains of New England. It was serene and peaceful. I was looking straight down on Buffalo Creek. This was one of the towns highlighted in the documentary about the tragedy known by most as "The Buffalo Creek Flood." In the spring of 1972, a wall of water and mud like none seen before or since came roaring down the hollow in the darkness, sweeping away everything in its path and causing the death of hundreds and destruction in the millions of dollars.

I had to stop for a moment and think of all those lives disrupted and destroyed by that horrible wall of water and mud. But being the tough mountain people that they are, they had rebuilt and were doing the best they could to put their lives back together. Why would they go back, you ask? It is simple, this is their home!

That bird was gone and there was no way to follow him up. Two or three times I thought I could leave the old grown up path and climb around the contour of the mountain to hit some likely looking spots. I was wrong. I could go 25 or 30 yards and then the mountain simply dropped away and all I could do was hang on and climb back up to the road. Being the gentleman that he is, Jared didn't once say "I told you so."

Jared Justice, Logan County native, poses high above the tiny hamlet of Buffalo Creek, where a black wall of mud, water and coal dust once swept away the town, killing hundreds. The mountains above these deep valleys are home to many grouse.

The dog was working well and we were finding birds. The cover was thick and most birds shot straight down the mountain as soon as they left the ground. I had noticed a lot of horse tracks and droppings as well as some sign of the wild boars that are in the area. Jared pointed out that a few wild horses in the mountains had been running lose for several years now. The haul roads we were on were unlike those up in the northern part of the state that are 20 to 50 yards wide. These seemed only wide enough for a truck to come out. But once in a while we would come to the point of the mountain where the road doubled back. Here, there would be a wide spot where the trucks could back up to turn. Most of the strip jobs were covered with autumn olive that appeared 20 years or so old. There were also some multiflora rose bushes but they had not hit that year and the birds were scattered.

Walking along one sharp ridge we saw Ginny on point ahead where there were a few scattered pines mixed in with the autumn olive. Jared went straight in behind the dog and I made a quick circle out to the side. When I was about even with the dog a big male grouse shot up and headed for the edge of the mountain. But I had a good shot and met him with a charge of 7 1/2's as he topped out. He cartwheeled down and Ginny started toward him. About that time he shot back up in the air and I hit him again with the left barrel of the 20 gauge. Tough birds, these grouse of the southern Appalachians, you ask? Not really, just a poor hit with the first shot. This "back into the air" gave us some concern later on, but that is a another story.

We took a few pictures of this big, red phase bird and then headed for the truck. We had circled the mountain and wound up back where we started. That afternoon we would hunt within sight of the world's largest dragline, a piece of machinery almost beyond belief. It has a boom 300 feet in length and a bucket large enough to put a tri-axle coal truck in! As Jared said, it can take the top of a mountain off in a very short time. The second place we hunted was higher than the first but we walked an old log road rather than a strip road. Jared had been in here the past week and had moved at least ten different grouse. The cover was a little different on this mountain. In addition to the autumn olive there was scattered mixed timber and even some wild grapes.

We were able to separate a little here as there were several small logging roads on the side of the mountain. Jared was on a little road above where I was fighting my way through a gnarled thicket. I looked out ahead just in time to see Tomba draw up into a high headed point. He was standing extremely high on both ends. I remember thinking he must really have this one nailed. I wanted Jared to see this beautiful picture, as sharing a moment like this with someone who really appreciates good dogs is more satisfying than shooting the grouse. I gave a soft whistle to get his attention. At the sound of my whistle, the birds started to get up all around Tomba and just out of good 20 gauge range. First, one in front of him. Then two more to his left, and another by a big tree top to the right. I was moving toward the dog when Jared yelled out that one just went back over his head. "There goes another," he yelled out again. Finally, two more got up below the dog and went sailing up over the high wall. As near as we could count there had been eight and maybe nine, different grouse. They were out feeding and the dog had gone right into the middle of them. With so much scent it was no wonder he was standing so high on both ends.

There are grouse in these southern coal fields, born of so much turmoil. It seems that most people only think of the Matewan shootout or the Buffalo Creek Flood when you mention Southern WV. But it is now known for a grouse population that can never be hunted out. They may come and go, as they do everywhere, but hunters, with their shotguns and dogs, will never hurt the population. Three years ago the population soared, and days of 25 and 30 flushes were common. The birds slid a little but have now started to rebound some, and pockets of grouse like Jared and I found are becoming more and more frequent. The lay of the land in Wyoming, Logan, Boone, McDowell and Raleigh Counties will prevent overhunting. Because of that, we are not afraid to highlight this five-county area.

It is no coincidence that these counties we are highlighting also hold the wild boar population of the state. The same remote, rugged, sparsely populated country that let the boars thrive brought good grouse populations. In fact, the first time hunter to the area would be well served to get maps of the boar area from the DNR and use these as maps to locate the old strip jobs to hunt grouse on. The first accounts of the area's high grouse population were from boar hunters from out of the area who were first to enter these southern mountains. When you disrupt the land, the new growth is just what grouse need to thrive. For forty years now the lands in the southern coal fields have been disrupted by the surface mining. The first areas mined are the most productive now as they were poorly reclaimed and planted with autumn olive, locust and other shrubs that grow well in poor soil.

Hunting here is a different proposition from the rest of the state. If you are hunting one of the old roads that runs around the mountain a long way from the top, it is a pretty good bet that the grouse will be on the edge of the road that borders the dropoff. The reason is, as soon as they flush, they will shoot out over the edge of the mountain and dive for the bottom. On the other hand, if you are hunting one of the roads that is near the top of the mountain, the birds often sit tight in against the highwall. These birds, when flushed, will often shoot up over the highwall and come to rest on the top of the ridge. If there is a way to get up over the highwall, these birds can be followed for a second flush.

All biologists that I have ever talked with say the same thing when it comes to grouse habitat. Grouse must have country where the ground has been disturbed. By this they mean that grouse thrive where we have had cutting, mining and fire. This pretty well describes much of this country in the Southern Coalfields. Timber cutting, surface mining and wildfires have created several thousand acres of prime grouse country.

The hunt just described took place in Logan County, but the same situation exists in Raleigh, Wyoming, Boone and McDowell counties in West Virginia, as well as much of the rest of Appalachia. If you were heading for Raleigh County, you would be best served by heading to its western section. We are talking here of the country west of Beckley, where much of this end of the county is old surface mining country. Larry Berry, biologist in charge of this section of the state, recommends hunting the cutover areas that are covered with brush ten to 15 years old.

Larry was also quick to point out that, while most attention is given to the benches where the surface mining took place, a great deal of country is available in the form of this cutover area. He pointed out that Georgia Pacific and Pocahontas Lands are two major timber producers that have thousands of acres open to the grouse hunter. If wanting to hunt some of this area, you would be well advised to hunt along the Wyoming-McDowell border. A little of this timber land has been leased but thousands of acres remain open to the hunter. No permit is needed unless so noted on the lands.

Here I might point out that, in this day of shrinking lands open to public hunting, these southern coalfield counties have almost no posted land. Posting of land simply isn't done in this section of the state. Hunting is deep-seated in southern WV's heritage and people there are used to hunting where they want to. The large land owners, and the coal and timber companies, have continued to allow this form of hunting. As long as hunters respect the land and the land owners, this luxury will continue. I never saw a posted or no trespassing sign the entire day that I hunted Logan County.

In discussing the area with Tom Dotson, biologist from McClintic, a couple of interesting comments were noted. Tom felt that an area mentioned

John Jezioro (right) and Dave Packard take a break to check a grouse taken in the rough little hills of eastern Ohio.

in print gets too much pressure, and that pinpointing a road or hollow eliminates the "hunting" we talk about. He likened it to going to the movies. He believed that hunters need to ferret out these covers on their own rather than being led to them. This was an interesting thought. While he agreed there is some good hunting in those counties, including Boone, which Tom works, he felt that people who come down to the area may not be prepared for the strenuous type hunting. The hunting along the ridge tops and the stripped off benches is easy. But once you leave the benches and ridge tops the land is extremely rough and steep. As Tom puts it, "the area is not for the weak of heart."

Since leaf drop comes a little later this far south, some of the best hunting can come later in the season. Grouse hunting and grouse hunters are becoming more popular in the Southern Coalfields as the grouse populations have been pretty stable for the past few years. Larry Berry mentioned that people down here hunt until the very end of the season. While you may see several out bowhunting the first part of the season, you rarely encounter another grouse hunter until after the deer season has ended.

A pair of good boots is a must in this steep, rough country. The boots you use here should have a fairly heavy mid sole and a good strong upper that fits the ankle area. When walking on such steep areas you need this type boot to prevent ankle turnovers. The bottom should have a good, rugged sole that will grip. As far as upper garments, the same you use elsewhere will work. The only requirement is that they should really be able to turn the brush.

A light, fast handling, naturally pointing gun in 20, 16 or 12 gauge will work fine. If hunting over a pointing dog, imp. cyl. and mod. chokes work well. If walking up your birds and jump-shooting them, an open choked gun might work best during the early part of the season when visibility is limited. As the foliage comes off a tighter choked gun may be the ticket as birds get up farther from the gun and you can see them farther. Good conditioning will make the hunt much more enjoyable.

If you are really willing to work for your grouse, this is the place for you and your dog. This is no walk through the gentle aspen covers of the Lake States or across a high mountain pasture laced with thornapples and greenbrier. Steep, rough, rocky and thick narrow valleys and high ridges is what you will find in Southern Appalachia. This section of the state continues to hold the highest populations of grouse according to state brood reports and hunting accounts. I am glad I had the opportunity to experience it with someone who so dearly loves and understands the area and its people. I will go back, but only after the dogs and me both take a little rest.

Grouse In The Land Of Turmoil

"If you want grouse, go to where man has dug, plundered, pillaged and burned." That profound statement was made many years ago by West Virginia biologist Jim Ruckel, and was racing through my mind as I stood looking at the boulder-strewn, upside-down country that lay before me. Jim was talking about what might be done to mother earth as a management tool. Granted, his words seemed a little harsh at the time, but his point was well made. His statement was made during a time when timbering and surface mining in Appalachia were under great attack and no one could see any good from such devastation. No one but a few farsighted biologists, that is. They knew that to maintain good grouse habitat we must cut timber and disturb the earth's surface. Surface mining does both, and encourages new growth in the form of shrubs and plants. The same result of surface mining for coal in Appalachia occurred from mining of iron ore and even gravel in the Lake States and Canada. For several years now we have ferreted out these old mining sites whenever we are in grouse country.

This is what brought Jack Barrette and I to this old, abandoned gravel mining operation in Ontario, Canada last fall. This was the seventh day of our annual grouse hunting pilgrimage, starting in Michigan's upper Peninsula, then up through the Iron range of Minnesota. Now we were staring out over a vast, defunct gravel mining operation in Ontario. The day before, we had split up and hunted some of our traditional types of cover. We walked the old clover-covered roads and hunted through expanses of aspen and birch. Problem was, everyone else appeared to have hunted the same roads and popple stands before we got there. We found a few birds but many more bird remains. As is the custom in much of the northern grouse range, hunters will shoot a grouse and then rip out the breast of the bird and discard the rest of the body, wings, tails and entrails, usually at the spot of the kill.

That night, with a little map reconnaissance, we located some old mining operations that had long ago petered out. Some, we were told, were iron mines and some were huge gravel operations that provided base for railroad beds and highways across this part of Canada. Not only did such operations create acres of disturbed land, but also miles of access roads that led in and out of the sites. These old roads, like the actual mining sites, had long ago grown over with shrubs, clover and popple.

We found the area to be just as we expected. The mining operation had been abandoned several years ago and the entire area was dotted with little islands of spruce and popple. A mixture of grasses and shrubs filled in between the trees. Sprinkled all through the area were bunches of waxy, red mountain ash and fuzzy, little tomato-like rose hips. The area gave the appearance of a huge amphitheater. Surrounding the entire covert was a high rim of shiny black rocks that you might see on the moon. The rocks and boulders gave the land a hard look except for the beautiful stands of mixed cover highlighted by splashes of dark green spruce.

I was running Pixie, my Elhew pointer, and Jack had his little dynamo setter, Dotty, with him. Casting them into the covert we followed, keeping track of their movements by flashes of white and the soft tinkle of their bells. I was swept up in that half daydream mode that overcomes us as we walk through beautiful cover, with good dogs, enjoying just being alive and feeling blessed to be free and uninhibited. Jack brought me back to reality with a soft whistle and a hand signal, indicating Dotty was on point up ahead.

He started in her direction as I made a quick, half circle that would bring me in from the side. Snaking my way through the thick underbrush I soon spotted the pointing dog. Her frozen stare was fixed on a scarlet clump of brush hanging heavy with rose hips. I whispered for Jack to get into position while I worked closer to the dog. As I moved I could hear Pixie coming on the scene through the tall grass on the left. As she passed me I whispered a soft "whoa" that brought her to a stop. She knows the drill well and immediately spotted the pointing dog.

She stiffened into an intense back as I eased past her. Nothing happened until I ducked low to go under a fallen tree. That's all it took. The grouse thundered out low then soared for the tree tops. His path took him in a semicircle that brought him back high over Jack's head. I saw him tracking the bird when he recoiled from the kick of the 16 gauge Bernardelli sidelock double. The bird sideslipped, dead in the air, then crashed down through a tall birch with a shower of leaves and twigs.

Dotty was first to the bird, but it was Pixie who delivered it to my hand. I was actually stunned at the brilliant colors of the bird. I called to Jack and we took a moment to admire the colors of this large cock grouse. It was a gray phase bird but the colors were much more vibrant, more distinct and more contrasting than any I had seen before. The blacks and grays were actually vivid, deep and rich rather than blending into each other. All of this was highlighted by the biggest, reddish-brown ruff either of us had ever seen. Only an upland game bird can retain such beauty after death. Because of such splendor I must always take a moment to smooth and straighten the ruffled feathers before carefully placing a bird in the game bag.

We continued to work across the floor of the pit until we reached the high wall that signaled the end of this part of the mining operation. Here there was a mixture of thick tag alder, birch and the occasional spruce. At the base of the wall surrounding most mining operations the ground will usually be moist, if not wet, from seepage. The damp earth found here is conducive to growing tag alder, birch and a mixture of thick grasses, providing both food and cover for grouse in a small area.

The dogs were working along the foot of the wall when both bells fell silent. Without a word Jack and I both began to slide between the thick stands of alder until I saw two separate patches of white among the black boughs of the tangled tag alder. I could also see patches of orange to my left as Jack closed on the dogs. I felt the bird would either go straight up over the wall, giving Jack a good shot, or come out to the right crossing in front of me.

I stopped and Jack signaled that he would continue on to the dogs. Jack's Dotty was holding steady in this divided find. Eyes bulging, nostrils sucking in and flaring out, the dogs were side by side and four or five feet apart. I herd the grouse begin that nervous peep-peep-peep that they often make as they are about to flush. I felt my fingers tighten on the straight grip of the 28 gauge double just as a blur of gray wings shot into the air. He was fighting to clear the grasp of the alders when I mounted the gun. Once clear he made the fatal mistake of hooking back to the right.

His flight brought him to me as the high-house #7 comes to the skeet shooter. As the barrels of the 28 overtook him, in a fast swing, I jerked the front trigger of the skeet #1 barrel. Hit almost head on by 3/4 ounces of hard 9's, his momentum carried him six or eight feet farther ahead where he crashed into the trunk of a mountain ash, tumbling in a shower of leaves and berries.

The dogs were also tracking his flight, and again Pixie was quick to retrieve to hand. With half of a flaming sun hanging on the far end of the covert we finished the afternoon in the gravel pit with six more birds moved and two more bagged while not another hunter was seen.

The next morning dawned pale and gray with a promise of rain. With a little back tacking and circling we finally found the gravel road into an abandoned mine. The ghostly white cement abutments and the huge piles of ebony rocks floated in and out of the fog, and were all that remained of what used to be a thriving operation. Like the gravel pit the day before, this area was scarred and torn into shredded strips of cover separated by huge windrows of boulders exposed by the mining.

This iron ore mine was similar to a coal strip mine with vertical walls stacked high with loose rocks and boulders from the size of a football to the size of a small Volkswagen. Even though the earth had been scooped deep to the ore rock, there were areas where enough soil remained to support nice stands of birch, aspen and spruce. The higher knolls were dotted with rose hips and some of the trees were bent low with the heaviest crop of mountain ash berries I had ever seen.

First one dog and then the other would find a grouse nestled in one of the little pockets of cover that were sprinkled about the old mine tailings. Until the snow drove us out at noon we enjoyed excellent dog work and great shooting, but there is always one piece of dog work that sticks in your mind as you exit a covert.

Jack was deep in the covert with Dotty, and I was walking the edge of an expressway like haul road while Pixie worked the steep sidehill below me. The slope was strewn with old logs, rocks, birch clumps and a few dark green spruce trees for color. I had a good view as Pixie worked up and down the hill. Suddenly she was not moving. The good ones never seem to ease into a point, but instead simply become transfixed to the earth. You can be watching but never really see the dog stop. She was stretched as tight as a banjo string looking right up at the road that I was on. Between us was a small bramble of mixed shrubs and grasses with a big bush of rose hips at the center. The grouse had to be in that tangle. I signaled for Jack to ease toward the dog. He knew that I wanted him to go in for the flush while I remained on the open road for a good shot. I was using him, but good hunting buddies take turns and it all balances out. There would be no way he could get a shot so he put his head down and marched toward the dog. When he was ten yards from Pixie the bird lost its nerve and shot out low in front of Jack and Pixie.

I was ready, and when he arched up over the 40-foot-wide road I had him skylined. He seemed to hang there for a moment, tail flared and twisted as he used it for a rudder to make his abrupt turn. I could clearly see his shiny dark eye and all the wildness that it held. The shot was easy, and Pixie was under him all the way and on him before he could flutter. We stopped for a photo or two and to look out over this vanquished land that was to the liking of grouse, hunters and dogs.

Grouse hunting continues to grow in popularity as the Lake States cycle appears headed into another high. During the last high cycle, friends of

Our grouse take us far and wide. Here, Jack Barnett takes a moment to admire the biggest, most beautiful red ruffed Ontario grouse we ever saw.

mine found themselves getting to more famous Wisconsin coverts at daylight to beat other hunters to the spot.

I refuse to get involved in that type of hunting. Granted, most of these traditional type coverts, whether they are in Appalachia, the Lake States or Canada, are pretty pristine and an absolute pleasure to follow your dog through. On the other hand, the old mined areas are often ugly, jumbled piles of earth and rock, twisted and turned upside-down and sometimes a nightmare to walk through. What they do have is miles of unhunted cover that holds the bird we love so much. In these areas it is simply too rough for the hunters to ever over hunt the grouse. Grouse have adapted to these plundered and pillaged areas but many hunters are reluctant to leave the beauty of their traditional upland swales. What is it they say about pain and gain?

Hunting these old mined out areas works from deep in Appalachia to the far reaches of Canada. That aside, these areas maintain a constant grouse population that doesn't seem to fluctuate as much as in other areas.

It takes Mother Nature several years to heal the wounds where man lays open the earth. Because of the time needed in this healing process, look for those areas that were abandoned at least 10 to 15 years ago. They are not hard to spot, just look for areas where man had dug, pillaged, cut and burned. If you are in grouse country the birds will have already found it.

CHAPTER 7

"ELHEW DON QUIXOTE"

As they might say on Broadway "Is that a name for a dog or what?" Well, in this case, Elhew Don Quixote is the name of a dog, and what a dog! I first met him nine years ago after George had picked him up at Bob Wehle's Elhew kennel. Now at 12 weeks of age it was already obvious that he was destined to be something very special to all of us. Like the literary Don Quixote, my friend George is somewhat of a visionary when it comes to seeing a pup's future. And like Don Quixote, George looks at them as an idealist, seeing only what he wanted to see, not what might really be there. But in Quixote the dog's case, this is where the comparisons end.

The liver and white pup, all elbows and feet, grew into exactly what George wanted him to be and into what all seekers of good dogs want. Soft, liver colored ears and a broad, royal forehead. If you wanted to show someone a prime specimen of what a true Elhew pointer was supposed to look like, you would take them to see Quixote. At 12 weeks he found four grouse we had hanging behind the cabin in Michigan's Upper Peninsula. He carried them one by one and laid them on the front porch. When someone would go outside, Quixote would pick one up and stand there holding it as if to say "Look at these wonderful things I found back there in the woods. Aren't they great?"

Quixote went on to become one of the greatest bird dogs George had ever raised, the one by which all others are measured. His legacy is prancing in my kennel right now, as well as in kennels from Mexico to Manitoba, Canada. His offspring are hunting quail in Mexico and Texas as well as chukkars in Washington. They are pointing grouse and woodcock here in Appalachia and all through the Lake States. At least these are the ones we know about.

For you see, there are many others who are chasing chickens on various farms. They are moving sheep and cattle from one pasture to another in Montana. Quixote's pups are chasing cats through the streets of Wakefield up in Manitoba and lie in their master's dens in Flint, Michigan.

You see, Quixote never felt that he had to breed only those selected bitches brought to him to carry on the great tradition of this thing we call bird hunting. To the contrary, he felt God had given him something special, and he should share it with every warm blooded creature he could. He was right. God had given him something special. In fact it was two things special. One was given him the ability to become a great bird dog, and to pass on those genes to produce other great bird dogs. This he accomplished, and you could tell by the look in his eye that he knew he had and was satisfied. It was the second gift he had been given that bothered him by what he felt was a lack of fulfillment or accomplishment. Quixote was "a Stud."

In every sense of the word he was a stud: big, beautiful, proud, independent, confident and endowed to the point that most men would hang their head in shame or embarrassment. Quixote felt that his mission in life was to breed everything that needed bred or wanted bred, and even those that didn't. While he died feeling a lack of accomplishment, it certainly wasn't from lack of trying.

Quixote had the run of every house, farm, kennel, lodge and sleepy little hamlet that George happened to be near while hunting. George is a free spirit. Accordingly he felt that his dog should be a free spirit, unshackled and unrestrained. George has complete trust in mankind and never felt that anyone would ever harm free-roaming Quixote. So, day or night, Quixote was left to romance the country until bed time. And romance it he did.

The routine was that after the hunt, he was fed and watered, and then free to see what might be close at hand that needed serviced. Because of Quixote I have this thing about the word "service." Every time that someone tells me they simply want to give "me the best possible service" they can I get this instant picture of a great liver and white pointer standing there with a wide grin on his face.

Well, as time went on, Quixote's fame preceded him throughout the country where we hunt birds. He became a legend in his own time. He remained famous for producing great bird dogs and servicing all he could. I always accused Quixote of not being particularly true or choosy to his own species but George only laughed it off.

My suspicions were vindicated while hunting a big covert over in Minnesota one warm afternoon in mid October. Quixote was working ahead, and I saw him enter into a little island of thick brush. All of a sudden, the bell quit, the wind died, and there was not a rustle in the leaves. "On point," I was thinking, as I hurried ahead 50 yards to the edge of the thicket. Just as I got there I was hit in the face with the familiar fragrance of skunk. As George neared I whispered to him that I feared Quixote had gotten into a skunk. George agreed and mentioned that he killed them when he found them.

We stood and listened but there was no ruckus coming from the thicket. All I could detect was a sort of prancing of feet in the dry bracken ferns. In a minute Quixote exited the thicket with the strong smell of skunk engulfing him. Then I heard the sound of running feet. I eased forward just enough to see into the cover.

There, not thirty feet away went a very big, and very alive, skunk. To this day it is the only skunk I have ever seen running, or walking, with its tail sucked up tight between its legs against its belly. I pointed this out to George but he insisted that Quixote killed them all. If I live to be a hundred I will never be convinced that Quixote was trying to kill the skunk! What I am sure of is the following episode in Quixote's life as I witnessed it and documented it for all time.

By now we had etched in stone that Quixote was to be the foundation of our breeding program. George had given me a lovely little female and, at four "Pixie" had displayed all the characteristics we wanted in our dogs. She was a true "people dog," one that felt she should be with you. She had a choke bored nose and was a natural backing dog. A good, soft mouthed retriever with a natural ground coverage that suited her perfectly to the grouse woods. We felt that if we bred her back to her father, Quixote, we could double up on all those great characteristics that both dogs had.

It was the middle of February when Pixie's time came around. Naturally George was off hunting somewhere. I got word to him, and in a day or two Quixote was on a plane from South Texas. Beverly and I drove three hours in a blinding snowstorm to reach Pittsburgh just as the plane was unloading. We rushed up to the baggage counter to get Quixote only to find that he wasn't there. We were a little frantic as they began to backtrack the flight. In a while a nice young lady came over to tell us not to worry. She assured us that this was indeed Quixote's flight but instead of Pittsburgh, Quixote was resting in Cincinnati, Ohio. Well, in another three hours here he came, appearing to be a little frazzled, and a bit bewildered, by his extended trip around the country

We extracted him from his crate, told him what a great dog he was and led him to the blanket in the back seat for his ride home to West Virginia. As we stated earlier he never met a stranger and was always at home no matter where he was. Our home was no different.

Across the street from us lived a dog I virtually hated until the day they took him away. Butler, a big yellow lab, was as worthless as teats on a boar hog. The only reason for being allowed to live was that he happened to be the pet of our neighbor's two wonderful little girls whom we all dearly loved. For as long as Butler lived, we planted new shrubs every year.

His routine was to come out of his house every morning, cross to our side of the street and relieve himself at the base of our mailbox pole and newly planted shrub. Every time I mowed the grass I had to get a shovel and remove the droppings from around the bushes before the cutter blades slung the mess all over the yard. In addition to this bad habit, Butler had another. No matter who came to our house he would run out at them, back hair bristling, teeth exposed and acting as if he would eat them alive. He once jumped into the open truck of a friend whose small son was terrified by his actions. On that occasion I tried to kill him with an ax handle, but I missed. Fortunately for all concerned he never bit any of my friends. He did bite the U.P.S. man, but I wasn't particularly fond of that guy myself.

Every dog in the neighborhood was afraid of Butler. He intimidated them all. All except Magic. Magic was our son Frankie's pet Doberman. He was as prime a specimen of his breed as Quixote was of his. The Good Lord never made a friendlier Doberman than Magic. The kids played with and rode him. He never had an ill bone in his body, but like me he hated Butler with a burning passion. He had good reason.

I never trust a German shepherd or a Doberman. No matter how lovable they are, I always fear that split second when they could turn on a child and inflict a terrible bite. Because of this, Magic was kept on a long, sliding wire in the back yard. Butler, of course, was allowed to roam the neighborhood wreaking havoc on everything and everyone. He would slip up to the edge of our house and peek around the corner to see if Magic was in his box. If he was Butler would silently ease up and grab Magic's feed pan and run back just far enough to where the Doberman's chain wouldn't reach. He then proceeded to wolf down the food while poor Magic watched. This went on for years and I often threatened to release Magic, but Beverly told me not to.

Stoney, an Elhew pointer grandson of Don Quixote shows all the style and class of his breeding on the first woodcock he ever encountered.

Well, I didn't have to. A swivel snap will only take so much pressure before it lets go. Sometime in the night Magic must have made a great lunge against the chain. I was looking out of the kitchen window that fateful morning when I saw the saga unfold. Magic was standing just out of reach of his feed pan that he must have moved during the night. I will always think that he planned it that way. The feed pan was where Butler used to drag it and finish Magic's food. Magic was standing beside his chain that was hanging from the wire as it always did when he was snapped to it.

I was watching, when Butler walked up and saw that the food pan was out of Magic's reach. Then he saw Magic standing beside the chain he has always been hooked to. Butler boldly walked up to the feed pan and started to gulp down Magic's food. He stopped and sort of snarled at Magic. Guess what? If you are a coon hunter you can picture what happened next. If you are not, let me try to describe it. In one blinding motion Magic had him. That great, 75 pound black dog had what looked like a limp piece of golden fur in his mouth shaking it for all he was worth. I knew from his grip that in a few seconds there would be no more Butler.

That didn't really bother me, but the thought of having to tell those little girls did. I raced to the door and into the yard just in time to release a very limp dog and watch it go crawling home. I snapped a new swivel on the chain and Magic lay down as if nothing had happened. I remembered thinking that this should teach Butler a very important lesson. It didn't. In a couple of days he was right back being the scourge of the neighborhood. I threatened to let Magic loose to finish the job, but good judgment prevented it:; not my good judgment, but Beverly's.

But on that first morning of Quixote's arrival Butler was the farthest thing from my mind when I let Quixote out for his morning survey of his new home and neighborhood. I had gone back to the kitchen, just poured a cup of coffee and was waiting for the toaster to pop when I heard the growl. I looked out of the kitchen window and there came Butler right at Quixote with that terribly intimidating posture that the yellow dog was famous for. I figured the mother of all dog fights was about to begin and was sort of frozen in my tracks on point. What had me baffled was the calm demeanor that Quixote displayed. I had watched him in several similar situations over the years, and he never backed down. Most encounters ended in the opponent being bluffed out of the fight. .

Maybe it was the plane ride, being isolated from other dogs for such a long period of time. Maybe it was simply that he already had a plan for this male bully of the neighborhood. Or maybe Quixote didn't know, or care, that Butler was a male. Now that I reflect on what happened next it could have been a moment when Quixote felt moved by the second of God's great gifts to him. He seemed to have an expression that said, "Could this be one that I have missed as I traveled around the country?"

Quixote's calm manner must have lulled Butler into a false sense of well being. He walked right up into the face of the great pointer and began to snarl and expose his teeth. Quixote didn't appear impressed at all with the exposing of the teeth. He seemed to be trying to look behind Butler to see what else might be exposed. I was watching, but can't really say how it happened. With the speed of a grouse leaving the ground, Quixote made his move. In one flash he reached out with a great foreleg, wrapped it around Butler's ribs and flipped his backside into him where he quickly then wrapped the other foreleg around the stunned yellow lab.

Just as quickly he began to execute the right he felt was God given. It is hard to imagine a 60 pound pointer trying to breed a 40 pound, male yellow lab but there it was for all to see. The snarl on Butler's face was now replaced with a look of bewilderment and dismay. That big yellow head full of snarling teeth was now sucked down tight into his shoulders. The only thing exposed was the tip of his nose. His back was humped up, and he was trying for all he was worth to suck his tail in tight against his belly, but Quixote would have none of that. If a picture is worth a thousand words, there stood a complete manuscript.

So stunned was Butler that he was catatonic. Quixote could do anything he wanted to him, and he was trying. The look of bewilderment on Butler's face was now changing to one of embarrassment and then shame. I was enjoying the show when Beverly came into the kitchen and saw what was going on. She insisted I get out there and save poor Butler from such a humiliating experience. I agreed and rushed to Butler's rescue as soon as I finished my coffee and the second bagel. I don't know if Quixote really got the job done. Only he and Butler knew for sure. I don't even know if it is possible. It made no difference because job done or not Butler streaked for home as soon as I got him released.

I have seen dogs run fast before but I have never seen one run so low to the ground! He ran right into the side of his owners' Mercedes and bounced back ten feet. When he got his legs under him he didn't go around either end of the car, but instead went under it, squirting out the other side like an otter.

Quixote was with us for another month, and it was two months after that before Butler even ventured to our side of the street. Like his master, Quixote was one of a kind. And like his master there will never be another. Thank God for letting me know them both!

So You Want A Grouse Dog?

"Frank, this is John Foster Evans calling. I am a grouse hunter like you, and I have read most of what you have written about grouse hunting. I have decided I am going to get myself a grouse dog and wanted to ask you where to get it, how to train it, and will it also be good to use on quail, woodcock, pheasants and maybe huns and sharptails. I want to get a dog like Sally, Candy and Ginny, you know, the ones you describe in your book Of Guns and Dogs and Men."

All this came forth after I had answered the phone and barely got "hello" out of my mouth. If you are a writer you will get many such calls and you have an obligation to do the best you can to answer the questions and give what help your experience will allow. Above all, you must be truthful. This means you must say some things the caller doesn't want to hear. With this in mind, I began to question the aspiring grouse hunter on the other end of the line.

The first question I ask is how often do you get to hunt? If the caller says he hunts once every other Saturday, except days when there is a top rated team playing, my answer is short and simple. One, you don't really need a pointing dog. And two, you will never have a true grouse dog if you do get a dog to work with. John assured me that this was not the case with him. He pointed out that he hunted at least twice a week during the WV grouse season as well as spending 10 days a year in Minnesota hunting grouse and woodcock

He went on to explain that his present dog, a flushing dog, just didn't seem to produce enough shots on grouse. He did well on woodcock and pretty good on pheasants, but he really felt he should have a pointing dog and wanted to get a GROUSE DOG.

I asked what he expected this grouse dog to do? He replied that he expected it to be always in sight, not more that 40 or 50 yards away, and to find at least 50% of the grouse that he would flush is a day. His grouse dog should point most of these so that he could shoot them. This was going to be easy, for you see, John had no idea what a true grouse dog is, and therefore, would be satisfied with much less. He simply wanted a bird dog that would point some grouse and let him shoot some over the points. What he was describing is what most consider a grouse dog to be.

After 35 years of following pointing dogs through the grouse coverts from Appalachia through the Lake States, into Canada and back again, let me tell you what a grouse dog is. First, he is more a specialist than any other dog we use in the pursuit of game birds. His closest second in being

By careful linebreeding we got Tomba, a grouse dog in every sense of the word.

a true specialist is the pheasant dog, one who actually knows how to work running cock birds into a solid point and hold them for the shot.

Over the years I have heard countless stories of hunters as they explained their most recent hunts. Somewhere in the conversation usually comes the phrase “we shot 90 grouse over Old Sport last season. When questioned a little further, it usually became evident that what they meant was that they shot 90 grouse while Old Sport was along for the day. Some of the birds he pointed, some he flushed and chased, some he bumped and some he just happened to be in the same covert with. Truly they were flying somewhere over Old Sport most of the time.

First of all let me say most inexperienced hunters place too much emphasis on the dog’s range. There is a big difference between range and self hunting. A good dog may cover a lot of ground, be out of sight for a minute or so but still check back to see where you are headed. The dog who becomes a great grouse dog is one that covers a lot of ground and will become a great bird finder. He doesn’t have to run out of the country but simply covers all the likely looking spots as you walk along. Pattern is another quality that many get wrapped up in. What good does it do for a dog to quarter back and forth in front of you when the best cover all lies above you on the hillside or below you in the bottom?

Here in Appalachia, our mountains and hills are broken up by what we call benches or flats. These benches or flats run along the side of the mountains and vary in size. Some may be as little as ten yards while others may be 50 yards. Because the mountains are so steep these are the only places where the hunter can comfortably walk. Here also is where the grape vines grow and climb the timber.

In hunting these mountains the hunter walks one bench while his dog works the one he is walking on and very often the one below and the one above. If the dog simply quartered back and forth in front of the gunner, like many would have you believe he should, he would find only the birds you yourself would flush. The great grouse dogs are not the mechanical robots many would describe. The great ones are like their masters, free spirits, self thinkers, able to figure out where the birds are and go there to look for them.

Good grouse dogs are born, not trained, to be great grouse dogs. We trainers simply reinforce some traits that we recognize and keep the dog in the grouse coverts. There are many things that we can’t train a grouse dog to do. We can’t train him to work a running grouse into a solid point. This is a trait the dog learns himself. He learns to work running grouse through some genetic trait passed on to him or her by other great dogs in their bloodline. The grouse dog has to have brains, if in fact, dogs have thinking brains. He will learn on his own how close he can get to a grouse before it flushes. He will learn that a grouse is less tolerant than a quail, a woodcock and even an early season hunt or sharptail.

The great grouse dog will never reach that zenith unless he or she has that most important prerequisite, an excellent nose. Dogs with average noses will find and point woodcock and even quail but will run over grouse scent until they are too close, resulting in a flush. You have all heard stories of dogs that stopped, threw their heads into the wind and then went stiff legged into the wind for 30 or 40 yards and stopped on a point with a grouse pinned ahead. Many of these are true and I have seen it more than you might believe.

I will tell you this after many years of observations. A dog knows when he has a great smeller, and he will use his nose more. If you watch a dog with a good nose you will see that he doesn't run up to every clump and stick his nose into it for scent. Instead he will hit the edges down wind and go to the next cover. He will often stop and throw his head into the air and test the currents. They seem to realize there is nothing there. These are the things we can't train them to do.

The same goes for learning where to look. The great ones will only need a few encounters. They won't need 500 contacts with grouse to make a grouse dog as some have written. A true grouse dog will hit every clump of greenbrier, grape tangle, witch- hazel brush, hawthorn tree and tag alder clump that he sees once he has found a few grouse in these types of cover. Here you can give them a proper start with their early training.

They hit all the likely looking spots by covering a lot of ground. Some dogs simply run and some hunt. There is a difference and you must be able to tell the difference. A grouse dog will hit the patches ahead of you as well as on the right and left. He will also hit those out to the side, on top of the ridge and in the hollow. And contrary to some writing, he will occasionally get behind you and point birds in cover that have let you walk by. He is simply everywhere but never really out of contact. He will be circling you constantly to keep track of your direction and position. He will be thinking nothing but grouse.

This "being everywhere" was brought home by Sally, the first of three great grouse dogs that have owned me. The first two years we had her we had to hunt a great part of the season in snow or not hunt at all. During those early years, we tried to flush every grouse in the covert and walked to each clump of good looking cover we saw. What became exceedingly clear was that every time we went to a piece of cover, Sally had already been there. Her tracks were around that cover and she was gone on to the next.

Hunting with a great grouse dog can be a very relaxing experience. You can walk along at a leisurely pace while the dog searches out the covert. There is very little brush busting involved when hunting with a good one.

The dog that possesses the traits described here would probably do an admirable job on most any game bird we hunt. To have a great grouse dog I feel you must yourself be a specialist on grouse. I will take it a step further and tell you that the great ones are usually found in the one-dog, one-man combination. Together these become what George Bird Evans described as deadly combinations on grouse. In my country grouse are "the birds" just as in the south quail are "the birds."

I have stated before that we use the same dogs on grouse, woodcock, quail, sharptails and huns. I must confess that our true grouse dogs are specialists and are only hunted on grouse and woodcock because their ranges overlap so much. We might hunt one of the grouse dogs for a day or two on quail, but they are hunted on grouse exclusively 98% of the time. When they hit the ground they are thinking grouse and where to find them.

The dogs we have identified as having what it takes to be grouse dogs are kept in the grouse cover for their training. By this I mean that once they have displayed that exceptional nose, the desire to please, the busy ground work pattern that takes them everywhere but never on a straight line, or out of the country, and the higher-than-normal head carriage, they are taken out of the training fields and placed in the grouse thickets for their training. If you want a grouse dog, a specialist, why would you continue his training in a wide open field?

This is one major reason why so many have trouble with range. They train and work their dogs only in an open field where the dog can see them and keep contact for several hundred yards. This would be fine if we hunted grouse in open fields but we don't. Because of this we move the training of the grouse dogs into the thickets. They are kept in the thickets until they are ready to go into the true grouse cover. It makes little sense to plant pigeons or quail in a clump of grass in a wide open football field if you expect the dog to learn and recognize grouse cover.

This is one of the few areas you can help develop the grouse dog you seek. It takes more time, but plant your birds in grouse cover. Set your traps behind logs, in clumps of greenbrier, grapevines, tag alder or whatever type of cover you expect to find grouse in when hunting. If the dog has what it takes, he will start to check out all these likely looking spots on his own.

It makes no difference if you hunt in the Lake States, Appalachia or the far west, it takes a very special dog to earn the title of "Grouse Dog."

So as we search for this elusive thing called a grouse dog, how do we recognize it when we see it and what do we do with it after we find it? First watch for the pup that seems to want to be with you. He will be the one in front of you and under your feet while his littermates are elsewhere. Don't worry about size. I have seen great ones that were both big and small. Look for the one who seems to carry his head at least above the back-line. I have never seen a great one that went around with his head on the ground like a beagle. Some of these have made excellent woodcock dogs and have pointed a few grouse that would tolerate a close approach, but dogs pointing and working foot scent seldom make great grouse dogs.

As you sort the pups watch for the one who seems to hit the scent of the planted bird from the greatest distance and wants to point as soon as he hits it. You don't want one that wants to get a little closer for a better smell before pointing. If the dog has to get on top of the bird to lock up, look for another prospect.

Plant your birds in birdy looking places. Watch for the pup who goes to the same spot once he has located a bird there before. The good ones will go there every time you turn them loose because they remember the bird was there before. Now move the planted bird to other similar looking spots.

The grouse dog will start to set up a line of search going from one to the next until he finds the bird.

How will you know what you have? When the training is done and you have hunted him for a couple seasons you will know if you have a grouse dog or not. The true measure will come when you can walk along behind the dog and every time you go to a likely looking piece of cover you will find his tracks already there. You won't have to call him to put him into a piece of cover, he will already have checked it out and gone to the next.

When, at the end of the day, you stop to tally up your flushes and find that you had 14 flushes, and of the 14 Old Sport had points on ten and was working two others that didn't hold, you are getting close. When you come of the mountain without moving a single bird it was because there were none there. Now you have a grouse dog! Take care of him, and don't hunt him on those crafty, old, running roosters. Keep him in the grouse coverts for the rest of his life.

Whenever you find yourself in a group talking about grouse dogs beware of the individual who spouts off that if you want a grouse dog you had better get a setter or maybe a pointer or a Brittany or shorthair as that one particular breed is the best for grouse hunting. That person has just identified himself or herself as someone of very little experience in the grouse coverts with a grouse dog. That person has just announced that he or she is someone with tunnel vision and a bad case of kennel blindness! Let me tell you that there are great grouse dogs in all of the pointing breeds.

CHAPTER 8

BASEBALL, APPLE PIE, ICE CREAM, CHEVROLET AND QUAIL HUNTING

A Tradition, Sport and a Way of Life in America

I am a grouse hunter by circumstance rather than choice. I was born and raised in grouse country and this was the bird to hunt. We all become many things because we are told at an early age this is what we are. You become a Democrat or Republican because that is what your parents are. You are a Protestant, Catholic or Jewish for the same reasons. These positions do at times change as our experiences and education broaden. These changes are not always good, but becoming a quail hunter has been one of the great ones.

We hunt because we love the birds, but more because we love the dogs and the work they do. Quail offer an abundance of good, solid, enjoyable dog work that is rivaled by none. It is no accident that most field trails for pointing dogs are run on quail. Before we go farther let me say that, when I talk of quail, I am referring to the Bobwhite. He sits tight, flushes with a flurry, challenges the best wing shot, and is excellent on the table.

His appearance leans towards the subtle browns, tans, blacks and buffs of the more conservative tastes. Because of this, he always seems softer, more gentle than the pheasant and the grouse. He has been referred to for years as "Gentleman Bob." This may have been the case in times past, but like his homeplace coverts of the deep south, he has changed. He has moved from the vast fields of grass and weeds to take up residence at the edges of creeks, brush choked thickets and black timber. He has also changed where and how he feeds as well as where he loafs and rests.

To have the best possible dog work and shooting the quail hunter needs to be out early. Unless it is extremely cold, raining or snowing you should be out in the fields right after daylight. The birds will move about feeding for a short period before moving back into the heavier cover where they will rest until the evening feeding period. When the birds are feeding there is much more scent for the dogs to work with.

When they return to the resting cover for the midday siesta, the dogs often have to pass very close to the covey in order to pick up the scent. A quail hunter might be best served by hunting early and late and then resting during the two or three hours from eleven to two.

When hunting quail late in the afternoon some precaution must be taken to protect the remaining birds of a covey. First, never follow a covey, shooting the singles until there are only five or six birds left. They need six to eight to form a proper nesting ring to protect them from predators and furnish warmth through the night. Second, don't hunt them until dark as this may keep them from coveying up for the night. Again, predators and the cold night might claim the individual. Quail don't like to be alone and will do everything possible to regroup if you give them a chance.

The bobwhite quail has a split personality. On one hand he is a symbol of a slower, more gentle time, a time when gunners took pride in the guns, the dogs and the horses they used in the pursuit of their birds. On the other hand, he is tough, tenacious and a symbol of the American ability to adapt and prosper if given half a chance. Not to know quail hunting is not to know a part of the true bird hunting history and tradition of the American uplands.

Quail Shooting vs. Quail Hunting

"Frank, me and my buddies would love to go quail hunting but we don't think we can afford it. Besides, we aren't sure we would enjoy riding up to the dogs on point and then having someone else flush the birds while all we did was shoot. You see, we raise and train our own dogs and a big part of the hunt for us is to work these dogs we have spent so much time training."

This comment surprised me a lot and upset me a little. During The Sportsman's Show in Charleston, West Virginia, a large group of bird hunters from Ohio, Kentucky, West Virginia and Virginia had gathered to talk bird hunting, bird dogs and bird guns. As the conversation continued, it was apparent that this new generation of bird hunters was missing great hunting opportunities due to some misconceptions. Most of the quail hunting they had heard or read about presented the plantation shoots that are advertised in every bird hunting magazine. Just the mention of "quail hunting" conjures up visions of majestic pointers standing chest deep in golden grass scattered among the Piney Woods Country of the Deep South.

The continental breeds, such as this German shorthair owned by Steve George, find favor with many of the nation's hunters.

If you look hard enough you can see a perfectly matched pair of Georgia mules hitched to a grand old shooting wagon. Behind the uniformed driver sit two gunners, dressed to the hilt. What a grand picture they present. From their Wellies to the tweed shooting coats, complete with ties and matching pork pie hats, they stand for what quail shooting was in the South during the grand years.

The handler has now ridden up to the dogs on a beautiful Tennessee Walking Horse and dismounted. He motions for the gunners, who take their classic doubles from the leather lined gun box, to approach the point. When in position the handler flushes the covey and the gunners take one apiece from the small covey of about eight birds. The dogs make the retrieve, the handler places the birds in the bird box and the gunners remount the plush seats of the shooting wagon. This is quail shooting in its grandest tradition and God bless those who are fortunate enough to experience it and who also enjoy it. But it is not as many of us would have it. Some day I too will go on a quail shoot but for now I will hunt.

Many of today's gunners will never get the opportunity to enjoy a $300-$500 per day quail shoot. Many don't want to. Over the last several years, the pursuit of this noble sport has changed greatly. Quail numbers in some the traditional southern states have fallen drastically. Coupled with this has been the loss of big chunks of habitat. The result has been that many of the Plantations now offer quail shooting that supplements wild birds with liberated birds. These are great shoots and present a lot of opportunities that otherwise would not exist.

Several years ago our grouse hunting in the Appalachians also began to plummet, with low cycles lasting longer and not recovering to previous highs. When this happened the more adventurous of my generation took Horace Greeley's advice and headed west with our bird dogs. What we found was quail hunting unsurpassed in the south. From eastern Missouri to western Kansas, from southern Nebraska to southern Oklahoma the nation's Heartland opened its arms to the quail hunters.

The grouse hunters came from the mountains of eastern Kentucky, West Virginia, Pennsylvania, Ohio and Michigan. The quail hunters came from Arkansas, Georgia and the Carolinas, where their beloved birds had become a mere shadow of their former presence.

This mixture of ridge runners, rednecks and Yankees brought with them their method of hunting. The aristocrats of Europe, whose offspring settled much of the South, would look down on the hunting style of this group and refer to it as "Rough Shooting." No self respecting Brit would think of

Grouse dogs must be people dogs. They must want to be with you, hunt with and for you. Establishing this bond starts when they are born. Here, Mary Jo Jezioro plays with Old Drummer's Sir Lancelot (Lance), our third generation Elhew pointer.

leaving his shooting butt to follow a pointing dog. Instead he would prefer to stay in the butt and shoot the driven birds while his loader hands him first one and then the other of his matched Purdeys. Again there is nothing wrong with this. Different strokes for different folks!

For those who love the freedom to roam behind a pointing dog, this Rough Shooting in The Heartland is the ticket. Let me say here that, on the average, the best of the quail shooting in North America will occur in Texas and Old Mexico, but that is another story in itself. We are talking here of the opportunities open to the average hunter with average means.

The Heartland shooting we're talking about takes in Kansas, Missouri, southern Nebraska and northern Oklahoma. These areas have great wild quail shooting and offer the best chances to hunt both public and private land. On our first trip to Kansas we were complete strangers. We walked into a cafe in a small town early the second morning for breakfast. I noticed that the same group of eight farmers and ranchers were at the same table at the same time as the day before. I walked over and introduced myself and asked if they knew anyone who owned land in the area where my wife and I might hunt quail for a day or two. They looked at each other and laughed. Then one robust, friendly looking fellow spoke up.

"Well, there's about 50,000 acres sitting at this table and there are quail on most of it." I was surprised and apparently showed it. I mentioned that was more than we had time to walk and pointed out that we were not interested in seeing how many quail we could put in our sack but more interested in working the dogs.

The conversation grew as did the invitations to hunt on two of the farms at the table. Once those individuals saw we were careful, responsible hunters, access was obtained on other farms from the same group at the table. Over the years I have found that this same situation exists in every little farming community in this section of the Heartland, an area that I call "The Quail Belt." The crops are harvested, the fall planting done and the winter plowing finished when we go out in December. While a farmers work is never really done, they do experience a slack period during this time of year and meeting for coffee and breakfast is a Heartland tradition.

While there is good quail hunting over most of the four states I have mentioned, let me zero in on The Quail Belt. This will simply narrow down the area to go into if you are a complete stranger to the area. I-70 is your pipeline through the Quail Belt of The Heartland, from Columbia, Missouri west to Hays, Kansas. Seventy five miles north of this line will put you into some of the greatest of the Heartland shooting.

The end of the day, and Beverly checks the beautiful colors of a pair of wild Kansas quail.

The other two areas we have had good success in are north along the Nebraska border and south along the Oklahoma border. Between the Kansas border and Route 60, hunt from Miami west to the Blackwell area. Twenty five miles north and south of the border is good country. We also hunt 25 miles north and south of the Nebraska border from Falls City to McCook. The closer to McCook you get the more the quail and ringneck will overlap.

This is a big chunk of quail country to be sure, but really narrows down your search. To be more specific would do two things: First, it would betray the confidence of those who took me into their coverts. Second, it would eliminate a part of your hunt. To search and find a good area has always been exciting to me. To ferret out a nice farm loaded with quail is as exciting as bagging a limit there. If we eliminate this part of the hunt we are getting back into the quail "shooting" business. For those who have a hard time zeroing in on good cover, I will go one last step and tell you to hunt along the Republican River in Nebraska.

This was our eighth year to Kansas and the dogs were whimpering as we pulled up along the milo field. The milo had been harvested right up to the edges of the native grass on the west and to the edge of the black timber that lined the meandering creek on the east. Past experience has taught us that the quail will be along the edges of the timber after the first hour of daylight. They spend very little time in the open, since the vast amount of spilled grain, whether it be beans or milo, lets them fill up in a short period of time. Then it is back to the resting cover until the last hour of daylight, at which time they will go into the open fields again before roosting.

We would start the day with Pixie, our Elhew pointer, and Tomba, our English setter. Quail hunting in the Heartland presents many challenges, one of which is the constant wind. Today it was gusting to 35 miles per hour. Beverly pulled up her collar against the cold northwest wind and we cut the dogs loose. They have hunted here before and knew they were now in quail country.

They were scorching the edge with Pixie in the lead. There may be no prettier sight than watching a good pair of pointing dogs reach for the edges. They enjoy the freedom of the cover and realize that the boundaries are few and far between. A dog here needs to reach out and the boot polisher will furnish little, if any, excitement. There is a thrill, an unequaled feeling that overcomes a gunner as he walks 150 yards to his dog locked solid on his birds. There is always the anticipation of a wild flush and there occurs a little quickening of the step as the gap narrows.

I was watching Pixie as she floated effortlessly over the edge of the grass when Beverly brought me back to the reality at hand. "Tomba is standing abut 20 yards into the black timber near that dead tree." We started towards him and Pixie saw us change direction. She came roaring in and slid into a solid back when she spotted the big setter riveted to the black earth. What a picture! Two great specimens doing what they were bred and trained to do. The muscles of the pointer's forequarters rippled under her tight skin while the wind danced through the hair of the setter.

As I walked in I remember thinking, it doesn't get any better than this! Beverly was to the side with the camera and I had the vintage little Belgian Browning 20 gauge O/U ready to jump into action at the flush. I was even with Pixie now, the backing dog, and working towards Tomba another 20 yards ahead.

I could feel my hands tighten on the small grip of the Browning as I drew closer. Each step brought mixed thoughts. Have they walked away from the dog? Is this a nonproductive point? Could it have been an old ringneck rooster who has now left he country? Where are they ?

One more step and here they come! No matter how many times I experience a covey flush of wild bobwhites I get an extra surge of adrenaline. When that stops I will hang up the gun. I swung on a low, left bird, slapped the trigger as the barrels passed his beak, and saw him fold in a downy puff as the 1 oz. charge of eights centered him. At the same time I was aware of birds towering above the timber. I followed one with the second barrel, a miniature brown missile with a 35 mile hour wind behind him.

I began to overtake the high flyer from beneath. This shot, like a high house #8, is made by slapping the trigger as soon as you overtake the bird and continuing your swing. I pulled the trigger and sent a charge from the mod. barrel into the tops of the black timber. Problem was I never caught up with the quail. In fact, I was three feet behind him and simply couldn't move that fast. I knew what was coming next.

"Slowing down a little as you get older may dampen your quail hunting" came a comment from Beverly's direction. "It wasn't that, it was the dirt the wind blew in my eyes as I looked up" I quickly countered, as Tomba came racing back and stood waiting for me to take the beautiful little wild cock quail. There is nothing more beautiful, or faster flying through the timber, than a truly wild quail.

For the next ten days this scene was repeated time and time again, changing only when the bird that roared out from under the dog's noses was a big old rooster rather than a quail. We found from four to nine coveys of wild quail each day with anywhere from 12 to 25 or 30 birds in a covey. In addition, there were the wily old roosters to test our metal. This is more dog work and shooting than I've been able to get in an entire season the past few years in the grouse woods back home.

Quail Under Ice

Since man first emerged from his cave with his pointing jackal he has searched for greener pastures through which to follow his pointing canine. This continues today, and if you follow these old dogs long enough and far enough, you will encounter every condition imaginable. Modern day gunners are still going west searching for those coverts stacked tight with game birds. If you hunted the heartland in December of 1994, you encountered one of these imaginable conditions. It was called ice.

We were somewhere west of Lawrence, Kansas, when we noticed something different with the countryside. It was very shiny and bright. Closer examination showed that the countryside was encased in a clear sheet of ice. The trees, wires, branches, grass and fences were wrapped in a beautiful, diamond-like case.

At one of the local service stations we were told that the ice came about five days ago and no one really knew how it would affect the quail. Many feared the worst as similar conditions had wiped out entire populations in years past. The rest of the drive northwest seemed to be an eternity even though it was only about three hours. I had seen ice like this before in the Eastern Panhandle of WV and it had decimated the quail population. When the ground is covered like this for that long a period of time, the quail can't scratch for seeds and they will starve in short order.

We pulled into the motel after dark and began to unload and put the dogs on the tie out chain. I had a sick feeling as I examined the grass next to the motel. But when you come 1,200 miles to hunt quail and run your dogs you don't pack up and go home. We waited long for this yearly hunt and ice or no ice we would hunt the following morning.

We couldn't see or find another hunter in the motel. The clerk told us that the hunters that were there had left the day the ice started and no one had been out since. Sleep came hard that night. I wasn't as concerned about a bad trip as I was about the quail population being hurt for years to come. I was awake waiting for daylight when the alarm finally went off. It had been cold that night, in the teens, and no thawing had taken place.

Breakfast out of the way, we headed west to our favorite farm to start the hunt. I had planned to start two of our pups that morning but decided to go with two of the proven dogs. I didn't want to miss any quail and come away thinking the birds were not there when, in fact, the young dogs simply didn't find them. Tomba, our setter and Pixie, our pointer are as efficient a team as I have ever hunted behind and we have great confidence in their bird finding ability. They would get the call.

The author moves in on a point where a milo field borders a twisting black creek in classic Kansas quail country.

When we stopped at the harvested bean field and I got out to open the gate, I nearly fell as the bare ground was a sheet of ice. This gave new concern for the dogs. I know they have better traction with their pads and toenails than we have with our boots, but I still fear a fall that could injure or break a leg or hip. At first they walked about gingerly as if testing the traction. Soon they were bouncing around as if the ground was bare. That concern seemed to vanish, for the time being anyway.

This beanfield winds around a deep cut of a creek as it dissects the farm we were on. Traditionally, the birds feed on the beans and retreat to the thicket that surrounds both banks of the creek. The cover along these creeks looks black from a distance. The timber in this section of Kansas is thick, unyielding, sticky and hard on both man and dog. In addition, it is some of the best resting cover that the bobwhite can find. As we walked along the edge of the bean field I noticed that the ground cover under the timber was very sparse.

Closer examination showed that the ice had flattened the grass and there was really not much for a quail to hide under. We continued following the creek as it wound around the edge of the field but not a sign of a bird, not even an unproductive point to give a little confidence and reassurance. The dogs were cutting back and forth, in and out of the field and the timber without hesitation.

I was really getting concerned now and was expressing this concern to Beverly when she yelled "point!" Immediately I spotted both dogs standing at the edge of some heavy ice-encased grass in a bend of the creek. We moved ahead until we were both in a position for a shot. At first I thought the dogs might be backing each other as they sometimes do when one stops for a nature call and the other thinks he is pointing. Then the one going to the bathroom sees the other standing and he backs, or honors, him.

They usually figure it out in a minute or so and go about the business of finding birds. I stopped to record this beautiful sight on film. Quite a picture, those two locked into an intense point.

As I closed for the flush, if the birds were really there, I realized it was Tomba, the setter, who had the point and Pixie was backing him. He was looking right into a clump of Indian grass about three or four feet high that resembled long, golden stems of crystal as they stood glistening in the early morning sun. Passing the dogs I expected every step to bring a rush of wings but nothing happened. I stopped, looked back at Beverly, and stepped into the grass. It sounded as if glass was breaking as the pieces of the ice fell to the ground. That was all it took!

I had stepped right into the middle of a covey of about 25 birds. They were coming up all around me at the same time. With a year's lay off, and a Doubting Thomas attitude, they caught me completely by surprise. I swung on one big fat male in the middle but then dropped back to another one a little closer. He went behind a tree and I went to the right and picked another, but there were three more on the left. I was aware of Beverly's double cracking twice but I was handcuffed. I had committed the beginner's error. I was going to shoot them all and wound up shooting none.

If you have stepped into a covey of WILD quail you will understand, or at least I hope you will. I could tell I had a sheepish look on my face when I turned to face Beverly. "How many did you get from that big covey"

The author moves past the dogs to flush a single from the tall grass prairie.

came her smiling inquiry, knowing all the while that my gun was silent. "I couldn't shoot as the first ones were close to the dog and the next ones were going in your direction," I managed to blurt out excuse number 103 in the latest edition of The Quail Hunter's Handbook. Being the gracious hunting partner that she is, she just smiled and told the dogs to fetch the pair that she had folded. As I walked on ahead I heard her ask Tomba, loud enough to make sure I heard, if he had heard that weak excuse I had come up with. I never looked back.

As I walked on through the little patch of ice covered grass I noticed that the ground underneath was bare. The strong prairie grass had withstood the weight of the ice and formed a perfect hiding place for the quail. With this new knowledge we began to skirt the field edges and look for the little patches of grass that were scattered around the field at irregular intervals. Checking the birds Beverly had killed, we found that they were stuffed with soybeans. I walked on out into the field and, lo and behold, there were rows of beans sticking up through the ice. Here the beans were exposed and the quail could easily feed on them. I began to feel a little better about the plight of our little friends. With food in the fields and cover of the grass nearby the birds should be fine.

The creek and the field made a bend to the right. The dogs seemed to understand what was happening as they were now heading straight for the next big clump of grass, and bypassing the timber where they would normally hunt. I let them go even though they were ranging out a bit farther than I like. This is open country and even our grouse dogs will range a little farther than they would back home. Then again, if they didn't reach out and cover the ground we would miss a lot of good cover. Rounding the bend of the field we found both dogs stacked up on point. This time it was hard to tell who had hit the birds first.

Mentally I gave them credit for a divided find and motioned Beverly into position to shoot. I find it more and more enjoyable to watch someone else have a good shoot while I get great satisfaction out of a good photo. Believe me, it is much more difficult to get a good action shot than it is to shoot a quail. Three good shots taken, camera away and the dogs standing there, as if sculpted out of the prairie floor and embedded in it.

Nothing moving except the hair on the tip of Tomba's tail. These are the things that the gunner with pointing dogs can relish, while those who follow flushing dogs must see everything as a blur as there never seems to be a break in the action. I always get the feeling of urgency when following a flushing dog. That's why the Big Man made pointers and flushers; different strokes, folks.

Finally, Beverly asked if she should send out for lunch or if maybe I would go in and flush the birds so she could shoot another or two for the dogs. The birds must have been watching me as I only began to take a step in their direction when they exploded as only a covey of wild quail can. That whrrrrr of wings came as no surprise this time. I could plainly see the white heads of the three cock birds as they went out and away to the right as would the high house number two. I took the lead bird first and dropped back to the trailing bird as I do in sporting clays. The one ounce loads of eights from the 20 gauge double took both birds solidly. In the blink of an eye it was over and silent. The dogs came back with a beautiful cock bird apiece. I asked Beverly if she had forgotten to load her gun as I didn't

Beverly Jezioro tries to decide the proper approach to get the shot as Pixie and Tomba pin a covey of Kansas quail between them.

remember hearing her shoot. Her reply wasn't covered in any of the books I had read. It was original and well suited to the occasion but contained nothing about guns, dogs or shooting excuses.

The rest of the day was a repeat of this first hour. Adaptable and tough this little bird some call a gentleman. He has survived the harshness of the prairie for several generations. This year he knew to go to the bean fields and hide in the heavy grass for cover. This change in locations presented some of the best shooting and dog work we have ever had. It reminded me more of the old, traditional quail hunting scenes I have seen on those calendars of bygone years.

When I stopped for a moment to watch the sun come to rest on the prairie, I thought I saw them moving across the horizon. Two shooters with high leather boots wearing buttoned collars and shooting coats, stiff and straight, in the waist-high grass. They were following two magnificent pointers, one black and white and the other liver and white, who seemed to flow over the prairie, in and out of the native cheat grass. I almost wanted to wave, but before I could, the wind swirled the grass and they were gone. The ice had put the quail in the grass and we had enjoyed quail shooting as our grandfathers had enjoyed.

Nine big coveys were moved that first day. I am convinced we could have moved more had we stuck with the veteran dogs but that's not what we came for. To miss the great training available to the young dogs would almost be a sin. They don't learn anything in the kennels.

Even the pups soon learned to first search for the clumps of grass and then the quail that were near by. It was a strange sensation listening as they coursed through the ice. If you would close your eyes it almost sounded as if someone were playing a tiny, crystal symbol as the ice broke and fell to the ground.

What started out as a very iffy situation finished as one of the most memorable trips we have ever had to the prairie. There is no way for this humble scribe to describe the beauty that laid before us. As the wind stirred the grass, the ice would catch the different rays of the sun and set off a kaleidoscope of sparkles. It appeared as if the entire prairie were encased in one great, multifaceted diamond. And in the center of all this sat one of nature's true gems, "Gentleman Bob".

Quail in The Black Timber

Snaking their way through the golden milo stubble and fawn-colored soybean stems of the Kansas Prairie are thousands of serpent-like creeks choked with plum thickets, honey locust and Black Timber.

Dear Sirs:

"Please find enclosed your world's greatest, best, toughest, softest, bull-brier proof, shooting gloves I purchased from you three weeks ago. I got the gloves as I need a new pair, and since I was heading into the quail country of Kansas, Missouri and Nebraska, I felt the ones you had advertised were just the ticket. As you can see, both you and I were wrong.
Like many out here in the real world I hunt, and hunt hard, in rough country.

After only ten days in the Black Timber of Kansas the gloves are in shreds, as you can see. I can only think that the fellow who field tested the gloves before you put them in your catalog must have tested them on his way to the bank for his daily deposit. There I think they would be fine. Obviously, he never hunted true bird country. Please send me another pair as they are comfortable and I, too, will wear them to church on nice days."

We pulled into the pasture and parked. The dogs were let out while we gathered shells, collars, and vests. As I was assembling the 20 gauge Model 21, I was looking down into the bottom where the creek snaked its way through the grasslands and the milo fields.

The creek was a stark contrast as it twisted back and forth through the golden brown stocks of the milo that had already been harvested. The dogs were cut loose and we headed out through the pasture toward the milo stubble. What a picture! Two great pointing dogs tearing back and forth through the stubble. Two hunters following along with fast flying quail on everyone's mind. Caught out in the stubble the birds are not easy targets; wild quail never are, but they are easier than when they are in the Black Timber.

It was about noon and we really didn't expect to find any quail out in the open stubble, and we weren't disappointed. At midday we expect to find the birds inside the timber five to ten yards, depending on the depth of the timber. It was easy walking through the stubble as all you had to do was follow a row. The dogs weren't wasting much time in the open. They, too, knew that the birds are not in the open at midday. The dogs acted like they were hunting the stubble, but it was plain to see that they had their sights set on the timber along the creek ahead.

Ginny got there first, and the little black setter melted out of sight. At nine years of age she still hunts like a three year old for about three hours. She has what we call heart, and she has put it into her offspring. Pixie, our pointer was reaching out as there is a little jealousy between her and Ginny, always has been. Ginny was popping in and out as she headed upstream the way Pixie was headed. They didn't have to be guided into the wind. Like all good dogs they were following their noses.

The creek made a bend and the bank flattened out some and reached back into the timber for about 40 yards. We kept going towards where we last saw Ginny. When she didn't reappear in a minute or two we quickened our pace. When this dog doesn't check in you had better go look. Most of the time you find her stretched out as tight as a banjo string. This was no exception. The first thing I saw was her orange collar. The next thing was Pixie, standing tall and hard, in the background.

I have hunted in thick, sticky coverts all over the country, and can tell you that the Black Timber of The Heartland is about as tough as it gets. We all talk of the thick country we grouse hunt in, but I can assure you it is softer, thinner and much easier to get through it than the cover along the creeks and waterways of the Midwest's quail country. As we stood there sizing up the situation it became obvious that a clean shot would be nearly impossible. There was only one way into the dogs, straight at their rears.

I always prefer to come at the point from the side or front. This cuts down the angle of escape, often pinning the bird between the gunner and the dog. It is a wise bird that will double back low, over the dog. I knew where this covey would go and there was nothing I could do about it. I told Beverly to get ready while I ducked my head and plunged into the spiny mess. This black brush is unyielding. It simply doesn't bend. I literally bounced back a step. That commotion put the covey into the air and all we could do was watch and try to mark them down. A covey of 20 to 25 birds and not a shot fired! Unusual, you ask? Not at all. I have had days when I moved two or three coveys without a single shot. This covey bored into the thick timber toward the other side of the creek.

When we walked on through the timber I could see that the cover on the other side of the creek was very thin and only about 10 yards deep. If they didn't pitch down on the stream bank they had to overrun their cover and fly across a 500 yard wide pasture field, or dump into the pasture field which had short, scattered clumps of grass. Too good to be true, I thought, as I looked for a way to ford the creek. The bridge was really a beaver dam. Beverly took one look at the dam and the deep water on either side, and decided she would shoot the ones that came back across.

I coaxed the dogs down to the beaver dam and they followed me on across. They hit the bank and were gone up the other side while I virtually crawled up the steep, muddy bank. Just as I was about to clear the top, Beverly yelled from the other side that they were on point about 50 yards out in the open field. Standing up now I immediately saw them side by side in a divided find. Neither was moving a muscle and their intensity signaled that they had their bird nailed!

I whispered a soft whoa just to let them know I was coming. The field was wide open and covered with grass no more than knee deep. I quickly moved out to the right side and started in. They were fixed on a little tuft of Indian grass no more than ten feet in front of them. I watched for a moment and could see from the bend of the grass that the wind was directly in their searching noses. Reflexes took over and my grip tightened a little on the 20 gauge.

Two steps toward the dogs and out they came. First one and then two more. They bored straight away presenting easy shots. I took the first that came out and when the next two came, with just enough delay to recover from the recoil, I was in position and ready. The skeet two barrel centered him and he bounced on the prairie. Two minutes ago an entire covey exploded and not a shot presented. Now two easy shots, shots that you might expect to get in some of the traditional southern quail cover. The dogs made snappy retrieves and, after a few seconds of telling them what great dogs they were, we were off again heading up the big, grassy draw.

They were flowing in and out of the prairie grass and I was temporarily mesmerized by the natural beauty of the prairie. Some say it is drab and boring. I find it has an individual character all its own. It was good to be out of the timber, to experience the freedom the prairie country is famous for. The dogs and I were getting farther and farther away from the timber when they again swung into the wind and pointed. There they stood, skylined, two marble statues growing out of the little blue stem grass that surrounded them.

Pointing into the wind, the only movement was those searching nostrils that said "they are here, trust us." I moved up in anticipation of the fast flying single about to explode at their feet. The grass was thin, but search as I did, I couldn't see the single sitting in front of them. I wanted to get a photo of the quail in front of the dogs but this was not to be the time. I put the camera down and moved in to flush the bird.

When they went up I was in the middle of a large covey. I swung on the big brown headed hen that was sweeping to my left. She was barreling back toward the timber but as the barrels covered her I hit the trigger and saw her fold up. I was conscious of birds everywhere. I went after a big cock bird that was coming back over the dogs and hooking toward my right shoulder. "I will take him," I thought, but there, over to the left is a straight away and I dropped down on him just as two more went right by my face. I instinctively turned to follow them and take the straight away. They were dropping quickly and I knew I was over the bird when I mashed the trigger.

All this seemed to take a minute but it was a only few seconds. I heard a little chuckle from the other side of the creek and remembered I left a very important part of this hunting team on the other side. "Boy, did they handcuff you. Right out in the open where you said you hoped you would find a big covey someday. You let them get back into the timber," she finished. Realizing she had watched, I was searching for an excuse but none came. Finally I countered that I wanted them back in the timber where they at least had a chance. Another subdued chuckle and we headed together back up the creek.

Following the black timber deeper into the prairie, we rounded a little bend of the timber and froze. Looking down into a large tangle that surrounded a big, dead cottonwood tree, we saw the dogs stretched out, side by side, locked onto the jumble of briers, thorns and vines. While we were standing there deciding which way to approach the point, the birds flushed. It was another big covey of 20 to 25 birds. They bored deep into the black timber of the creek banks with only two or three ever clearing the tree tops.

The creek made a big, horseshoe bend creating a peninsula of land that was about 100 yards wide and 200 yards long. On the other side was a 60 acre field with two inch high wheat. It appeared the entire covey had pitched down into the big flat just ahead of us. With the dogs back under control after the flush, we began to ease into the black thicket. We had gone about 75 yards when Beverly said that the dogs were just ahead of her with their heads buried into a tuft of waist-high grass.

I told her to move on in and I would shoot if they came out into the woods where I stood. I saw her stiffen a little, gun at ready, as she began a slow, deliberate approach. She was beside the dogs now but nothing moved. It was obvious that the birds were buried into the washtub size tuft of grass in front of the dogs. She looked at me for direction and I motioned for her to step on into the grass. Being the good soldier that she is, she stepped into the grass, which then exploded into her face.

Instead of the crack of her 20 gauge the silence was pierced with a shrill, shriek of "oh my God," as one of the birds actually flew up along the front of her pants and coat, so close that she later said she could feel the wind from its wings. Needless to say, not a feather was ruffled by a shot. Once she regained her composure, we went on into the thicket.

The dogs were almost frantic from all the scent and the abundance of birds at hand. I called them in and sat down on an old cottonwood log for a moment to get them calmed down. In a few minutes they settled down, but kept looking on out into the flat ahead knowing that he birds were out there. With Beverly and the dogs ready, again we moved on.

This time it was I who saw the dogs on point. I wanted Beverly to get some shooting, and called her over. With the last flush still fresh in her mind she was a little nervous as she closed on the dogs. The ground cover was a little more open here with a covering of the short, briery bushes that bear tiny scarlet bunches of berries. Beverly was still 20 feet from the dogs when the bird broke cover. It shot straight away and she was on it quickly.

I saw it fold at her shot, and at the same time saw another quail flush away to her left. Swinging on that bird it too tumbled at the shot. It was close enough to a double that I gave her the benefit of the doubt. At this point we had to take a photo break to record the proud huntress with her brace of wild quail.

Each hunt has a moment which sticks in the hunter's mind above all else. Beverly's double was that moment until the next event. The following day we were working another stretch of the black timber when Tomba, our English setter vanished into the edge of the cover. Walking over to the edge I spotted him standing on his tiptoes, tall and handsome, with his nostrils flared wide sucking in the wonderful fragrance of wild quail.

Beverly decided this might be the perfect chance to record the flush on film and readied her camera as I drew closer to the dog. When I was about where I thought I should be for the flush I stopped for an instant and glanced back at Beverly to see if she was focused. That was a mistake. The birds must have been watching me, because they flushed the instant I glanced back.

It is hard enough to pick up individual birds when they are in the open, and almost impossible as I whirled back around and searched the branches for the rocketing brown birds. I was aware of several, blurry, blobs boring away into the dark timber at one time, but couldn't focus on any individual bird well enough to take the shot. Beverly advised that she had a great shot, and then inquired, without much subtlety, why I just stood there with my mouth open. Lost for words I could only say that I wanted to get them scattered so we could work on the singles. With that rather insufficient comeback we moved in the direction of the disappearing birds.

Tomba hunts hard and fast, and has the tight bored nose that prevents him from overrunning or bumping his birds. I was watching him rip through the cover when in a blur of movement, I saw him completely double up. His head was right beside his tail which was stiff and pointing at twelve o'clock. I wanted to get a picture of this and began to fumble with my camera. I had to set the light and focus and was taking longer than normal to get it just right in such poor light.

With one eye on the camera and the other on the dog, I noticed Tomba starting to waver a little. I was hurrying as fast as I could but it wasn't fast enough. As I watched Tomba began to weave back and forth but never took a step to right himself. Finally the position was so off balance that the dog simply flopped over and lay there in the grass on his side still doubled up in a semi-pointing position trying to hold up both his head and tail. I had to laugh out loud and this noise, with the commotion of his falling, was more than the bird could take.

I wanted this bird for Tomba more than any other I could remember him pointing on this trip. In one motion, I dropped the camera to dangle on the strap around my neck while mounting the 20 gauge double. In a state of panic, as I watched the bird disappearing out of range, I shot before the barrels had settled. I killed a nice, young locust tree with that shot as the quail was increasing the distance between us. I took that split second needed to set the bird on top of the barrels and mashed the trigger again just as the bird reached the creek bank. I saw him tumble over the bank as the shot charge of the skeet two barrel took him squarely.

Tomba was following the bird's flight and vanished over the bank as I watched. The next sound was that of splashing water. I hurried to the bank and looked over. There was a still fluttering quail, floundering on the surface of the deep pool, moving down stream with Tomba in hot pursuit. Finally the dog overtook the bird and scooped him up in his big, soft jaws. Making a turn that would rival a competition swimmer's, the dog was quickly digging his way back up the steep mudbank. Shaking himself violently to dry off I could only see the tiny feet of the quail sticking out of those big, hanging jaws. In a second, a very proud setter was standing at my side to deliver his hard earned trophy. Even though I didn't get this action on film, that picture will remain sharp and clear for as long as my mind will work.

Bob White, The Savior of The South

As I stood assembling the 28 gauge double, I had to take a moment to think of the true symbol of the South. Before us glistened a vast sea of waist high, golden broomsedge. Sprinkled across the grass were lonesome pines appearing as little green umbrellas. Standing guard over the entire savannah were towering, ancient oaks that have seen 300 hunting seasons pass among them; majestic mammoth trees, their sprawling tentacles oozing fluffy strands of silvery-green Spanish Moss.

At that moment, I realized just what it was that preserved this pristine tidal plantation that we were about to hunt. It wasn't just people with money, as there are many who can simply write a check. Instead it was men and women of vision and passion. Their vision was to see these stately, old plantations preserved for the enjoyment of many future generations. Their passion was hunting, more specifically, quail hunting.

When farming no longer supported operating rice and cotton plantations, the tax collectors and carpet baggers swarmed over the land like a plague of

Pixie and Tinker nail a covey in a small grass field above a Midwest bean field. The edges of such fields are ideal cover.

locusts, devouring everything in their path. Many plantations were divided into smaller tracts that became housing developments, shopping centers, parking lots and tourist attractions. Others were purchased as private shooting preserves by individuals and small groups. These individuals also found themselves faced with increasing tax burdens, to the point that they decided they also must sell. They could have sold to developers who would have covered the land with concrete, but instead they searched out those men and women who appreciated the land and its character.

They found the people and the backing they needed in the nation's quail hunters. While some will tell you the symbols of the south are glowing young maidens, cotton, stately mansions, manicured lawns, mint juleps and even grits, I must respectfully disagree. I am here to tell you the true symbols of the South are men and women who hunt and shoot, well bred walking horses, great strains of pointing dogs and the Bobwhite Quail. It is the love of this shooting life that has resurrected many of the South's vanishing plantations.

Quail, in much of their original range, have all but disappeared. I first sampled this great sport in West Virginia's Eastern Panhandle. There, on land made infamous by the events of the Civil War, tucked up tight against the Virginia and Maryland borders, were remnants of the great coveys that once flew across the tilled fields of small farms dotting the land. Quail hunting with good pointing dogs is as addictive as gun powder. Once you get it into your bloodstream you are hooked for life.

Raised in the rugged mountains of WV, I started bird hunting by chasing grouse up and down the gut-wrenching, lung-busting spine of The Appalachians. This is a hard, harsh land and I seem to attack the coverts when after grouse. On one side of the sidelocks I consider the ruffed grouse of Appalachia the wiliest of all birds for both hunter and pointing dog to bag fair and square. The grouse is sly, crafty, tough and tenacious, and I consider every one taken over a good staunch point to be a true trophy of the uplands.

On the other side of the sidelocks is the bobwhite quail. I approach quail hunting on the plantations with somewhat of an apologetic manner. I have always considered the bobwhite quail a soft and gentle bird, a bird that symbolizes the essence of hunting with pointing dogs. It is no accident that much of the early sporting art featured a pair of gunners, walking in knee high grass, as they approached a beautiful pair of pointing dogs that were locked solid onto a covey of quail. That scene was burned deeply into the minds of many of us who yearn to walk those same fields.

Over the past several years I have experienced great quail hunting in Kansas, Missouri and Nebraska. It was the kind of hunting I grew up with, the kind where we entered the brier-choked thickets early in the morning on foot, and walked until the setting sun cast its dark fingers across the milo fields and plum thickets.

Like the fox who couldn't reach the grapes, therefore deciding they were probably sour anyway, I had put the idea of a plantation hunt out of my mind saying that it was too much quail shooting and not enough quail hunting. Time went by and I secretly hid the visions I held of following my pointing dogs across large expanses of the South's lowland, quail country. As much as anything, I wanted to experience the feeling of walking through a part of American history and heritage that was foreign to me.

That opportunity came when George Burroughs invited Beverly and I to join him at Bray's Island Plantation for a few days' quail shooting. I went with no illusion of covey after covey of wild quail rising before the solid points of the dogs. To handle the pressure that a large shooting plantation gets, the birds must be released. Most of the plantations have learned that by putting birds out early, the quality of the shooting is enhanced. They also found that by keeping the birds in big, secluded flight pens, away from all human contact, the birds become very strong flyers and less tolerant of the gunners and the dogs. This conditioning of the birds presents nearly wild conditions.

Bray's Island is private and the epitome of a true, well preserved southern Plantation, similar to many other plantations in the U.S. Because of the excellent quail shooting, and the opportunity to talk and shoot with world renowned sporting clays instructor, John Higgins, we sprang at the opportunity.

The dogs were getting impatient and their whining brought me back to the moment at hand. I had come to Bray's Island Plantation as a guest of my old friend, and mentor. George, like many of the other members of Bray's, was drawn here by the quail hunting. The privacy, the golf, tennis and horseback riding were all great, but it was only the quail that interested George.

Three years ago George and I linebred my Elhew pointer, Pixie, back to her father, Elhew Don Quixote, a great bird dog owned by George. Like many others, my experience has shown that if you want the truest examples of the breed you must line breed. You must know, and study, the characteristics of the dogs to be bred. While line breeding will strengthen the good qualities that you want in a dog, it will also strengthen the other qualities in the dog, therefore you must be ready to accept all that is good and bad in the particular dogs you are breeding. Naturally, you should not line breed if you feel the undesirable qualities overshadow those you want to strengthen.

I had done this same type line breeding, father to daughter, twice before and was very satisfied with the results. This time was no different as, for all practical purposes, our Tinker was a clone of her mother Pixie. On this trip we would be running the results of that breeding. Both George's Bucky and my Tinker had already proven themselves in the grouse and woodcock coverts. In addition, this trip would give me an added opportunity to introduce seven month old Stoney to quail. Last year we bred Pixie to Bob Wehle's Elhew Mr.McGoo. Stoney, and the rest of the litter, are prime examples of what good breeding can achieve. He has already shown that he will be the one to be bred to Tinker to carry on this bloodline that has produced such outstanding grouse dogs for us.

On these extended trips I take four or five dogs as I enjoy watching a good pair of dogs work their country and handle their birds. We had parked in the middle of a 200 acre area, and agreed that George would hunt to the south and I to the north. Tomba and Tinker hit the ground at the same time, stuck their noses into the wind and began to slice the covert into quarters. I decided to carry my petite 28 gauge, Ugaretechea, Bill Hanus Bird gun and George opted only for a check cord as he is continually fine tuning his dogs, placing the actual shooting second to the dog work.

I watched the scattered pines and grass swallow George and turned to follow my own dogs. We were working a field that had a thin line of pines on the left side and big timber that disappeared into the swamp on the right. Tomba was coming back toward me when he wheeled and pointed into a little, brush choked ditch. Pixie rounded the end of the strip of cover, saw Tomba and immediately stopped to honor his point. There was no need to hurry and I took a moment to snap a few good pictures of these two beautiful dogs standing their birds. I remember thinking how they complemented the land with their flowing beauty and grace.

Neither dog moved and I began to circle to come in from the front of the dogs. I stopped about 10 yards from the dogs but nothing came out. Tomba's intensity told me the birds were in there and I moved toward his outstretched neck. Two steps toward his nose and the grass exploded with quail squirting in all directions at once. I picked up a big, conspicuous one, tracked him until the barrels passed his nose and mashed the trigger. I saw him fold and crash into a small pine, easy to mark down. Still swinging I picked up a late riser that was hooking hard back to the right. As soon as I touched the trigger I knew I was behind the bird and he sailed off untouched.

I took a moment to smooth and admire the feathers. While a bobwhite quail is not a gaudy, flamboyant bird its beauty comes through in soft, warm earth tones. Like a woodcock, they remind me of the subtle tweeds and plaids of an English, gentleman's shooting coat. Careful not to ruffle those aristocratic feathers, I tucked him into my game pouch and cast the dogs back into the wind.

The dogs were running hard and I tracked the glimpses of white, black and liver darting through the waist-high grass. They were moving toward the end of a long strip and I waited for them to exit the other end to see which direction we would take. As I stood waiting, a soft wind off the sun swayed the grass in long, rolling waves. I was almost lulled into a daydream when I realized the dogs hadn't come out from behind the strip of cover they were working. I started toward the end of the strip where it entered a thicket of briers.

Near the end of the strip I spotted both dogs standing side by side, like matched book ends, staring at a jumble of briers and grass that laid like a living blanket over the top of a fallen tree. I swung out to the right and made a fast half circle to put the tree between me and the dogs. I walked right up to the tree top and stopped but nothing happened. Neither dog blinked or moved its head, but instead seemed to intensify its stare into the brambles at my feet. Finally I kicked the trunk of the tree.

Quail must have been gathering here all day, as there were at least 20 in the air at the same time. Like a swarm of big bumble bees they were swirling around in all directions. For a few seconds I moved from one to another before settling down and tracking a big hen boring into the sun on my right. It was almost a going away shot and I thought I was shooting right at her when the gun went off, but the lead was ample and the bird crumpled. A pair of stragglers came out on the left and headed deeper into the thicket just as the barrels covered the one on the left. I pulled the trigger just as the quail went behind a tall, slender cedar tree.

Straining to see into the dark thicket I saw the bird bounce on the ground as he came out the other side. Pixie saw him also and was on him before he fluttered twice. The last 10 seconds or so had been a living blur of browns, blacks white and liver as birds and dogs moved in all directions, but now a serene calm fell over the savannah as Pixie and Tomba stood waiting to deliver their birds.

We were out of the thicket now and into an open field that had been mowed into strips. Between the strips were food plots of partridge pea, milo and dwarf corn, an ideal mix of cover and food. The dogs were racing down a long strip to the west where the sun hung like a giant fireball. Pixie hit her point so hard and fast that Tomba actually bumped into her, knocking her forward a couple of feet. She nearly went down but stayed in a crooked, low point. Being so close ,Tomba had birds in his nose also and was standing in a high, intense point.

Old friend and mentor, George Burroughs, lines up on a fast-flying quail in typical South Carolina low country cover. This is classic quail hunting in its traditional finest.

Not in any hurry, I was enjoying the picture of the dogs on point with that blazing sun as a backdrop. This covey wasn't as tolerant as the others we had encountered and, before I could get within 20 yards of the dogs, they shot out of the grass. Singles, pairs and stragglers, they all appeared to be flying faster than the other quail we had flushed during the day. I remember thinking that the dogs had found one of the truly wild coveys on the island. I struggled to get the barrels ahead of a big, white headed, cock bird that was going his own way. I forced the gun ahead of the bird and pulled the trigger. The bird was hit, but not hard. Pixie was after him and I took a stab at another, but only gave him a 28 gauge salute.

By the time I reloaded, Pixie was at my side with her bird. While all quail are lovely little creatures of the uplands, the colors of the wild ones are much more vivid, with distinct contrast between the different shades of brown, tans and black. Turning to locate Tomba I became aware of a cool wind on my face. There were no shadows now, and only a pink glow where he sun had been minutes before. How fast days come and go for the birdhunter. We can only take comfort in the thought that the Big Man will not deduct from a man's allotted time those hours spent with a gun and a dog.

As much a part of the shoot as the gun and the dog is the ambiance that seeps over the grounds of the plantation, like a warm delta fog, as the moon ushers in the night. There was just enough time for a quick shower before Beverly and I joined George and Betty in the formal dining room of the main house. The history of the Old South was everywhere as we entered the great room for a truly formal dinner. I had never seen so many forks at one sitting, and as I sat there counting them a very polite man came by and rescued me saying that I probably wouldn't need this one and that one over here.

The walls, floors and all trim were of stately, classic oak that had the color of wild clover honey. On the walls were three original paintings depicting quail shooting in its grandest tradition. The birds appeared to fly from the canvass as the dogs stood steady to flush. And what dogs they were, not the whippy, snippy-nosed slab sided pointers we often see today, but instead big-boned, deep chested, liver and white dogs with heads chiseled as if from granite, showing deep dished noses and heads with definite stops. If you looked close you could see their ribs move ever so slightly as their noses flared, filled with the sweet scent of quail.

The wine was soft and gentle but with enough character to be as distinctive as the quail over rice that was the center of the dinner. As we dined (in West Virginia we would have been eating) I found myself talking much quieter, almost subdued, as if I was afraid I would offend someone with a normal voice too loud for such devout gathering. Sitting there staring into the flickering, hissing flame that danced across the charred log, the sparks reminded me of quail shooting off in different directions as they had done before the dogs all day. I had come to the South to follow the dogs and experience quail shooting, and the South had overwhelmed me.

Sleep came hard that first night after the day's shooting. I felt myself jerk several times during the night as the dogs pointed and the quail got up all around them. I dreamed of matched Georgia mules and squeaky, high-seated wooden wagons, glistening, muscular pointers and beautiful silky setters. Following the dogs were gunners with handlebar mustaches, tweed coats, high leather boots, pork-pie hats and black, string ties. They carried trim, classic doubles and when they turned I was one of them!

Etiquette For Plantation Quail Hunting

With good numbers of birds there is no pressure to get a limit of quail, so these hunts take place in a very relaxed atmosphere. Because you are almost guaranteed of good, fast shooting, with an abundance of birds, there is more emphasis on the quality and quantity of good dog work. Under this condition, you can tone down your approach to the hunt. You don't have to approach the point in an aggressive manner. You can take turns shooting, with only two gunners approaching the dogs at a time. Shoot only those birds that go out on your side and don't shoot those that are hooking back behind. Don't shoot the low flyers for the safety of the dogs. I find a light 20 or 28 with 7 1/2's or 8's to be perfect for shooting over pointing dogs in this open cover. This is only a suggestion, as any gauge will work. Quail are the perfect game bird for pointing dogs, so above all, shoot only pointed birds; you owe them that respect.

CHAPTER 9

WOODCOCK, THE CONSTANT IN THE UPLANDS

Crossing the Blackwater, we turned into Ben Thompson's farm. Immediately, we knew we were in woodcock country. Both sides of the road were lined with tag alder and aspen. The soil was black, and the cattle had paths cleared all through the tag alders and on out into the scattered hawthorn.

While that was nearly 40 years ago, strange as it may seem, not much has changed along the road. The road now goes into Timberline, it is wider, paved and more heavily traveled. The clump of hawthorn on the right side of the road, near the fence, is where old Candy pointed her first woodcock. It still stands. I hear you saying, "I thought you just told us not much has changed in those 40 years."

Everything has changed except the habitat. The tag alders, the aspen and the haws are still there lining the road. The soil is still black, moist and sticky. The cattle are gone and you have to watch for the traffic. The cover is the same but older. And like it was that day 40 years ago, the woodcock still come. Move on north into the Canaan Valley and the cover is older, but the same. The same species are there. The aspen, the tag alder and the goldenrod still stand.

In the fall of 1995 I shot woodcock with my friend and hunting buddy, Jack Barnett, in a lovely little pocket of cover that George Burroughs named Woodcock Knoll. George named that cover nearly 25 years before Jack and I shot it in 1995. I also shot them at The Crock, another of Michigan's great covers that George named 25 years ago. These Michigan coverts have changed also, but the woodcock still come. They seem to tolerate a cover change better than any other game bird I know. The cover changes, but the soil stays the same. And since 98 % of the woodcock's diet is made up of earthworms, it is the soil that they depend on.

When woodcock habitat is lost, it is usually to what the chic like to call Urban Sprawl. They drain the wetlands and fill the swales to create more shopping malls. My God, how many malls do we actually need? That is progress, they tell me, and if the woodcock is displaced, so be it.

You see, the tiny woodcock doesn't play a major role in the game. While he is held in high a regard by those of us who know and hunt him, he is barely recognizable by those who don't. He is not flashy, like the gaudy pheasant. He is not a whirrrr of wings like the bobwhite, and he is not the challenge for the dogs and hunters that the ruffed grouse is. That aside, he is a true game bird in his own right, and without him the Upland Gunning Life that George Bird Evans so eloquently described many years ago would be incomplete.

I know I can still go into Grant and Tucker Counties here in West Virginia around the third weekend of October and I will find him in the same alder swamps and thornapple flats I did back in 1960. There are fewer now along the entire Atlantic Flyway, but they still come. My records show that from the third weekend in October to the week before Thanksgiving, depending on the weather, he will be in his favorite haunts.

In the 60's we had an early experimental woodcock season in Canaan Valley. The reason was that we wanted to prove that we truly had a nesting resident population of woodcock. The biologists knew it, but for some reason we had to document it. The season opened on Sept. 20th. or so, if my records are correct. I think the limit was five birds back then, and for a week those of us who hunted in the valley took limits of birds. It wasn't to prove that we could take a limit, it was just that there were a lot of birds there and no one seemed to consider that we should only shoot a couple a day to prove the existence of the native, resident nesting population.

I don't know if killing all those birds really had an adverse effect on the population or not. I do know that there were never as many in the early season after that. From that point on, the hunting pretty well depended on the arrival of the flight birds.

While talking of flight birds let me tell you of one neophyte woodcock hunter. This young hunter was full of energy, had a good dog and was destined to be a true woodcock hunter. Like all hunters, he had to start somewhere. He knew that Canaan Valley was the ultimate cover for woodcock back then and this is where he headed.

In the thick cover where woodcock live, the shots are often quick and close. Because of this, many hunters favor skeet chokes in their guns.

He didn't really know what type of cover he was looking for and thought you were supposed to hunt in the swamps. During this period, West Virginia biologists Joe Rieffenberger and Bob Kletzly were conducting an ongoing study of woodcock in the valley. They were night-lighting them as well as trying to catch them in little wire enclosures strung around the valley. Our young hunter was not noted for being bashful, and when he saw the two one afternoon near Ben Thompson's he stopped for information.

He was lamenting his sad story of no woodcock when Joe mentioned that things should pick up as soon as the flights arrived. This was just what

The first snow of the season often bunches the birds into staging areas as they prepare for the flight south. Finding these staging areas often results in 30 to 40 points in an afternoon, creating the best training opportunity you will ever find.

Jan Riffe moves in on Tinker's point as late season woodcock break from the cover of a small spruce tree. Some of the best gunning, and dog work, can come with the first soft wet snow of the season.

he was looking for. Now he at least knew they were on the way. In his youth and ignorance he asked the inevitable question. "Joe, what time do you expect the first flights to arrive?" Joe, in his gruff and serious manner, looked the young hunter in the eye, glanced at his watch, and announced that he expected the first flight around 7:35 the following morning. The young hunter was a little shocked and bewildered. Then I looked at Kletz and saw a wide smile spread across that gray, bearded face. When I looked back at Joe, he was busting to keep from laughing. From then on we have been friends, and the two were valuable sources of information on all aspects of the woodcock, his life, habits and habitat.

With much of the information gathered back then, Kletz went on to produce a very informative book entitled American Woodcock In West Virginia. It is a great little book and the most informative I have seen on woodcock. It was distributed by The West Virginia Dept. of Natural Resources and it's worth the effort of trying to dig one up.

If you do find one, you will see a picture of a pretty, smiling English setter on the fourth or fifth page. That was Old Drummer's Candy, one of the greatest grouse and woodcock dogs I ever hunted behind. I bred the litter she came out of with a nice old dog, Canaan Valley Zip, owned by my friend Doctor VanOrmer of Cumberland, Md. I took that picture at the big cherry tree that stands in the yard of Jim Compton's 'A' Frame cabin where the road starts around Cabin Mountain before dropping off into the valley.

During those early years there were very few who hunted the woodcock. Many wouldn't waste their time, as there were plenty of grouse to hunt. The woodcock remained a secret for many years. The fraternity was comprised of Biologists Walt Lesser, Jim Rawson, Bill Goudy, Bob Kletzly, and Joe Rieffenberger. There was George Bird Evans and his Old Hemlock Setters, Joe Smith and his great shorthairs from over in Elkins, Doctor VanOrmer and his buddy Dr. Cook from Cumberland, Maryland, Doctor Weimer, Tom Clawson and Roger Lundell from Buckhannon. These were the hunters who knew and loved the tiny woodcock.

Over the years, the grouse cycles came and went as did the bobwhite and his habitat. It was great hunting when the grouse cycle was high and the quail numbers up. They fluctuated greatly over the years, and they still do. The woodcock, on the other hand, has remained the one true constant in the upland shooting life. He comes and goes almost with the same regularity that Joe told our young hunter many years ago. He stops in the same covers year after year, and he is an excellent bird for training young grouse dogs.

He lives in the same coverts as the grouse, and our dogs learn to search for grouse when being trained on young woodcock. He has always played second fiddle to the grouse, king of all game birds, but if the grouse is truly King, our tiny timberdoodle has to be the Crown Prince of the uplands.

Woodcock In The Rain

Many years ago I decided I would not hunt grouse in the rain unless I was already out in the covert when a storm came up. If that happened, I would hunt my way back to the truck. At about the same time, I also realized that I enjoy hunting woodcock in a light, misty, intermittent shower. Many have been the days in woodcock country when we put on light rain gear, belled the dogs, and plunged into the islands of alder and aspen cover in search of woodcock.

While I have found grouse hard to find, and even harder to handle on dark, wet days, just the opposite is true for woodcock. Many days have been saved by our constant of the uplands. On such days, grouse seem to slink into the cover and hide under roots and logs. I have gone into proven grouse cover on a rainy day and emerged on the other side with not a flush. Go back again the next afternoon when the sun popped out and the birds were right where they should be.

On one such day in western Minnesota, Jan Riffe and I had just about given up when he walked into a pile of logs and practically stepped on a pair of hidden grouse that were buried deep under them. We began going to each and every downed log or pile of old stumps. Many produced a flush. The disturbing thing was that we had very little dog work. The birds must have been sitting there for some time with their feathers sucked in tight against their bodies. It appeared they were giving off very little scent. Unless the dog got very close to them, we watched time after time as the dog would pass a spot and we would then walk into it and flush a bird.

My experience with woodcock has been just the opposite. It makes no difference where you find him, the woodcock is predictable. We were going to hunt along Sand Run, at the base of Cabin Mountain in West Virginia's Canaan Valley. It was what I call a typical Canaan Day. It's a different world up there and you never really know what to expect. You get a good idea once you top Rich or Cheat Mountains, depending on which way you are coming into the valley. On this day there were broken clouds as we left Shaver's Fork, and the closer we got the denser the cloud cover got. Half way up the mountain from Dry Fork it was plain that we would be hunting in a misty fog, if we hunted at all.

It was early and we decided to go on through the valley and have a hot cup of coffee at the Warden's Hotel while we waited to see if there was any possibility of the weather clearing. At the hotel we ran into Doctors Cook and VanOrmer. They had come from Cumberland on their way into the other end of the valley up near Camp Seventy. There was no slinking into the covers back then. When you saw other hunters you knew, you stopped to exchange ideas and mention what your plans were for the day.

After the Big Man created woodcock, he created the 28-gauge and pointing dogs.

This accomplished, and no sign of a letup in the soft rain, our plans were finalized to hunt the day. We went in past the 'A' frame cabin and started the long descent into the valley. Maintenance of the road had long ago been abandoned by the power company that owned the mountain, the road and the valley. Soon we got to the spot where we wanted to park.

There was a tent camp of bow hunters there, and in passing conversation they said they had jumped several of those brown birds with the long bills as they went to and from their stands. The dog was anxious and appeared to recognize the country. We only had Sally then, but she was all that we needed. She was one of the few dogs we ever owned that was truly an all day dog. In fact, on our first trip to Minnesota we hunted her all day for six straight days. She only lived to be ten and I often wondered is she simply wore out before her time.

I was shooting a new 28 gauge Bernardelli double that I had built with woodcock in mind. I hated to put the little gun in the rain but that's what it was for. Peppe was using a beautiful Grade Four Ithica 12 gauge double that he got from Lloyd Ganoe's Estate. This was familiar country to the gun, as Lloyd had carried it through the valley for many years shooting grouse and woodcock. One of the most memorable photos I ever saw was of Lloyd with his gun, a young boy from Davis, and a bushel basket of grouse on the sidewalk of the Warden's Hotel. It was certainly an overkill but it attested to the numbers of grouse up there during that era. Lloyd used to get the young boy to go with him to carry the birds.

Between Sand Run and Cabin Mountain was ideal woodcock habitat for the migrating birds. It was made up of small stands of aspen, actually islands of aspen, in a sea of goldenrod. Scattered through it were little stands of soft maple. Many shallow hollows came down off the mountain to join Sand Run, and each had a small rill of a spring running through it. One of the pleasures of hunting this country in late October was walking up to one of the many pools and seeing a beautifully-colored brook trout on its spawning bed. This only added to the splendor of the country.

Pep and I started upstream with Sally casting between us. Everything was dripping wet, but the dog seemed to enjoy it since it was not a very cold rain. Her soft bell was truly music as the tone varied with her jumps and runs in and out of the cuts of the land. We were approaching the first little island of aspen when the bell went silent. I mentioned to Pep that we had a point, and we closed on the dog. We stood for a moment to enjoy the sight of Sally in her typical woodcock point.

She definitely had a different stance on woodcock and grouse. On woodcock she was stretched out low to the ground with neck and head extended. With grouse she was high on both ends. This was a woodcock and he was sitting tight. We agreed that Pep would take the shot and I would flush the bird.

This is the social aspect of woodcock hunting, the ability to discuss the moment as things don't usually happen in a flash of frenzied wing beats as they often do when grouse or quail hunting. I began a deliberate pace in to the dog. When I was two steps in front of her I spotted the woodcock sitting against a small bush. Our eyes met and I remembered thinking, in that spit second before he sprang into the air, that he appeared perfectly dry.

His was the typical spiraling woodcock flight as he fought to clear the 25 foot high aspens. Just as he leveled off, Pep centered him with the skeet barrel of the double. He was dead in the air and came down without a flutter. Sally was quick to deliver to hand, and we paused for a moment in the soft rain to admire the little bird. It was a big hen, fat and ready for her long journey south to spend the winter.

As he tucked the little bird into his game bag Pep commented how the lump felt good against his back, a burden looked forward to by the upland hunter. A little weight always seems to add to the day. About 75 yards farther up the stream we came to a landslide of rocks that split the aspen cover. Sally was already across and heading into a small glade where three

Another of the country's most dedicated wildlife biologists, Jim Hammill, standing, discusses grouse with George Burroughs who, at 80-plus years, says he has hunted through at least six grouse cycles.

or four pines stood mixed in with the aspen and alder. As we topped the bank, I saw her standing tall and proud looking into the little glade ahead.

The breeze was coming up out of the hollow and her stance spelled grouse. I signaled this to Pep and we started to circle the dog to get to the sides. I was just about to where I wanted to be when I heard the grouse start. Instinct took over and I was mounting the 28 even though I couldn't see the grouse. "Here he comes" came Peppe's shout from the other side of the cover. At the same instant I saw him, a big male, banking with tale fanned to make the turn. He went behind a small clump of aspens as the gun hit my shoulder. I continued the swing, and just as I passed the trees, there he was again going up the mountain from me.

As the barrels passed him I touched the front trigger and saw him cartwheel and plummet down through the brush. Sally saw him too and was after him. He was only wing tipped and his flopping and running was taking him into a clump of goldenrod. The chase was on and it ended quickly. Sally never returned a live bird in her entire life. She didn't tear them up, she simply dispatched them with a quick bite through the back. In a second she came out with the big male hanging out of one side of her moth and one wing over her left eye. On such a day I considered this grouse a true bonus bird.

The covert flattened out a little now and drew in tighter to the main run. Sally was off again as she always felt there was little time for anything but hunting when out in the uplands. It was only a minute or two when the bell again went silent. As we started over to her I heard two quick shots from far down the valley. I chuckled and told Pep that I would bet the doctors just missed one. Two such quick shots usually mean a miss, no matter who is shooting.

We came back to the business at hand as we closed on the low crouching dog. She was at the edge of a big piece of alder cover. The alders were only about eight feet high and there was a good deer trail running into them. Having taken the last shot I told Pep to get ready and I would go in to flush the bird. I could walk upright the first few feet but then had to bend to proceed. Just as I bent to go in I heard Sally's bell tinkle and turned to see her moving up also. "Birds running," I whispered back out to Pep.

This is one thing I have noticed on rainy days. It may be that, after a while, their spot lets them get wet or they may simply decide to walk around, but they do move on rainy days and it is not uncommon for the dog to relocate two or three times before actually pinning the bird. Sally was locked up again and I was bent double trying to get to the front of her for the flush. She swung her head toward me and I took a step just as the bird came up and out toward Pep.

"Coming at you," I yelled, as the bird went past my head. In a second or two I heard two shots as if they were from a semi-autoloader. I laughed and yelled out again. "I'll bet you a dollar you missed." "No takers here," came his reply. He explained that he couldn't shoot at first as the bird was near me. Then it bored right at him. Instead of waiting to let it go past and get out to where the pattern could open, he shot much too quick. His first shot had cut an aspen branch and the second had bored a hole in the rain as the woodcock whistled away on down the valley behind us. After the second

Early season woodcock hunting takes the gunner into some of the prettiest fall coverts in the Lake States.

shot, and while he stood there with an empty gun, the bird straightened out and flew straight away with plenty of time for a shot.

Sally knew the bird was gone and was off again to find another one. All three of us were wet now, but it made no difference. The hunting was good and the birds were holding well. The rain continued and we plunged deeper into the cover. Point after point took us farther from the truck. Sally was having a field day and we were getting shot after shot at solidly pointed birds. That afternoon was like so many others I have enjoyed on rainy, foggy days in the uplands.

We never found another grouse that day but we did take limits of woodcock before making the turn and starting back down the valley. The birds were plentiful then and the limit in the Atlantic Flyway was five. We recorded 43 flushes that afternoon and shot only solidly pointed birds. Woodcock were put here for pointing dogs and there is never a reason to simply jump shoot them unless you are doing so over a flushing dog such as a springer.

Even then, I feel the gunner is missing the essence of the bird by taking it in the rush and flurry that comes when following a flushing dog. Then again, who am I to say what is proper. Different strokes, folks! As long as

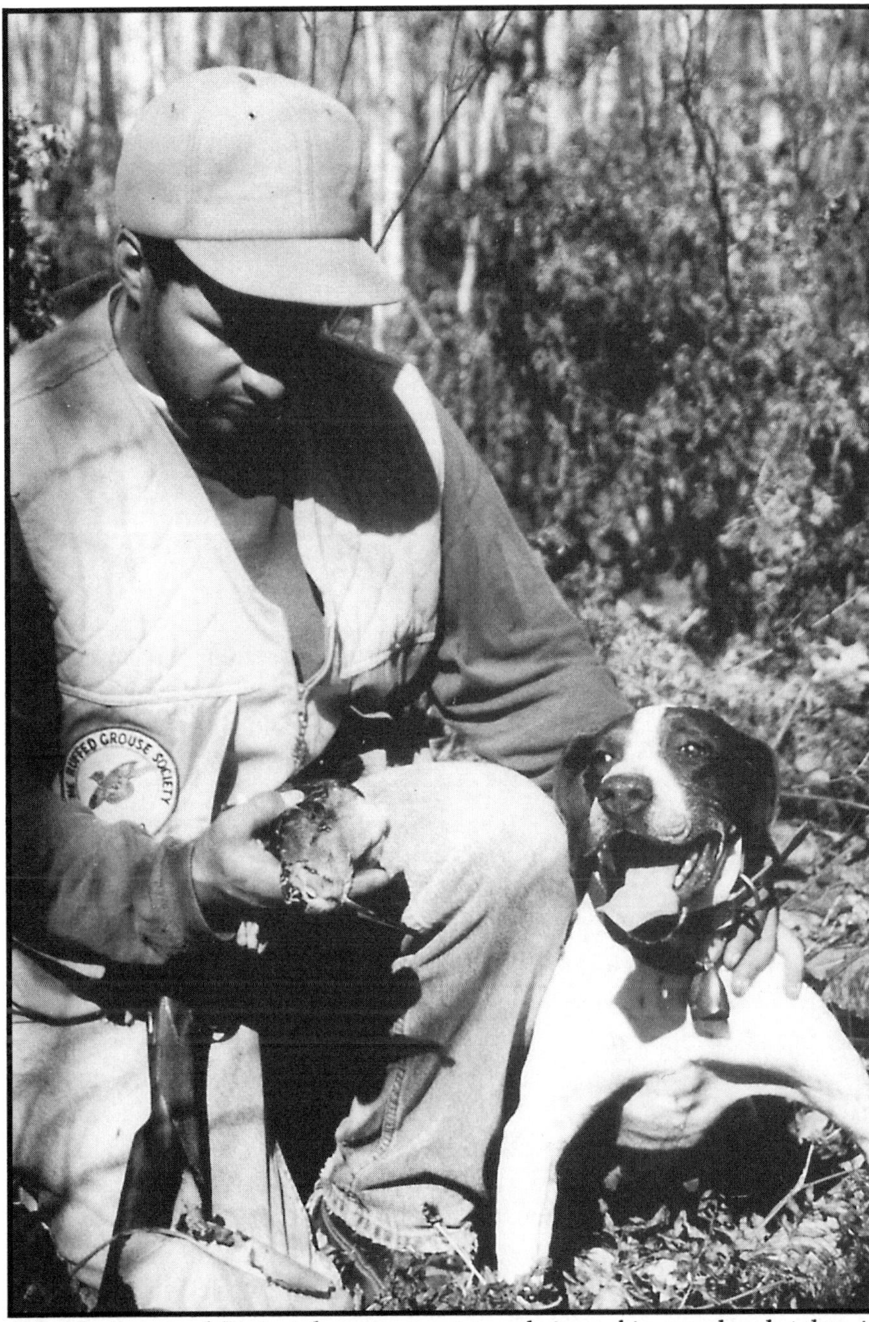

John Jezioro and Pixie take a moment to admire a big woodcock taken in Michigan's Upper Peninsula.

he is given the respect a true game bird is given, and as long as we see that he has adequate cover throughout his range, I feel the woodcock will always be the one true constant in our upland gunning.

Going Into The Thick Of Things

"Can you see the dog?" I half yelled, half whispered. "No, but I heard her last near that little island of aspen in front of you," came son John's reply. As fast and as quietly as possible, I started working my way in that direction. We were hunting woodcock in a dog-hair-thick covert so choked with aspen whips that most of the time I found myself walking sideways. I continued through the knee high bracken fern for another 25 yards, but still no sign of Pixie.

The little Ellhew pointer was on point but I couldn't see her. John was making his way toward me when I heard a single, soft tinkle note from Pixie's bell. I motioned to John and moved forward. There, not ten yards from me I spotted a patch of Pixie's orange collar through the brown leaves of the frost burnt ferns.

I whispered for John to get ready as I worked forward for the flush. As I neared Pixie she rushed forward five yards and slammed back on point. Both John and I moved forward again, and again the dog rushed forward only to relocate with an intense point. It was obvious the woodcock was running under the standing bracken fern. Contrary to what many hunters of limited experience have written, woodcock definitely run, especially when the ferns are still standing. At that time the birds will often walk or run away from the pointing dog undetected under the canopy of ferns. Pixie was now pointing into the last tangle of aspen and bracken fern before the cover was dissected by a meandering, little backwater brook.

At that point we were standing in thick aspen and tag alder, and about an inch of squishy, oozing muck. All we needed to add to the picture was a few fresh cow flops and we could have been standing in woodcock heaven. John held his position and I bent double to work my way to the last little island of dry ground that the dog was pointing toward. That break in my cadence sent the woodcock into the air. The same writers who wrote that woodcock don't run also said that they always spiral up, corkscrew fashion, then level off and fly straight away. Guess what?

This bird had not read the books. Instead of a slow spiral flight up through the open, it bored away, not more than six feet off the ground, darting around and through the picket-fence-like tree trunks. Still bent double, with my chin touching my knees, instinct kicked in as I tried to mount my gun, only to hit myself over the right eye with the barrels. I remember thinking I was glad I had the light 28 bore instead of the heavier 20. The blow sent most of me reeling backward, all except for my foot which failed to pull free from the black muck I was standing in. The best I could manage was a feeble, "shoot him John," just as I sat back in the quagmire.

From John's direction I heard a "whack" as metal smacked wood. Then, "bang, bang, damn." With a Herculean heave I dislodged the stuck foot but the boot didn't budge. The picture of a 200 lb. man hopping through a swamp on one foot while holding his eye with one hand and his gun with the other is not a pretty sight. I was doing fine until Pixie came zipping through the alders to see what sort of animal was breaking brush. She was barreling through the same tunnel I was in. Before I could manage a "whoa" she brushed by me. As I started falling backward again I pivoted on one foot and reached for an overhanging alder limb.

I would have been OK if that branch wasn't rotten! Spinning, twisting and lurching forward off balance, my weight was too much. Back down into the muck I went. This time only my left side went into the soup as I was able to hold my gun up and keep the sock on my right foot dry. I was amazed at how many different insects were still alive in the mud and now were buzzing around my head. In a few minutes I was able to beat the mosquitoes and gnats out of my eyes enough to see John standing over me.

After he was able to stop laughing he explained that, as I yelled for him to shoot the woodcock, he looked up to see the bird, bill straight out, coming at him like a winged dart. He ducked as it passed, turned and swung his gun smacking a small aspen. Getting by the tree he then fired two quick shots as the bird sailed on unscathed. As we talked, I freed my boot from the sucking goo, and we pushed on.

Before we go any farther let me address those of you out there who are saying that if we'd have had a beeper on Pixie we would have found her much more quickly. You are right. The beeper collars that pulse an audible "point" signal are time savers in locating a dog. But time to me, when I am in the coverts, is like time to a hog; it makes no difference! I enjoy every minute, and the anticipation I experience when searching for the pointing dog adds extra excitement to the hunt. I am not really interested in rushing from one point to the next to see how quickly I can locate the dog and pocket the bird. It may take me two minutes instead of one, and I get to appreciate the dog standing his point all that time. And if the bird flies away before I find the dog, so what?

As I have said before, the beeper collars are too space-age for me. I go into the coverts to escape much of today's electrified world. I don't want a cell phone, fax machine, electronic guidance systems or video-like electronic beepers surrounding me. What I do enjoy is the tranquility and silence, interrupted only by the lonesome tinkle of a little sleigh bell, the handiwork of some old craftsman. It's the same feeling I get when I carry the little 20 gauge Model 21 or the vintage Browning Superposed instead of the mass produced, machine stamped repeaters. Different drummers, and strokes, folks!!

We eased out of this part of the covert and followed Pixie into a large island of mature aspen. Even though she was hidden by the waist-high bracken fern, we could track her movements by the bell and moving ferns. Suddenly, we realized she had stopped again in front of John.

I told John to move in while I attempted a photo. This time the bird decided not to run. John was almost at Pixie's side when the woodcock sprang from under the ferns. John was caught in mid stride, surrounded by 15 foot high aspen whips. Being the athlete that he is, he sidestepped, ducked, and came up swinging. At the crack of his 20 gauge S/S the bird collapsed, falling in a shower of golden aspen leaves. Pixie made a quick return and we took a moment to admire the colors in the feathers of this great, little game bird of the alder bogs.

Moving from the top of the little hill we entered into a vast bowl shaped like an amphitheater. It was a clear cut coming back in solid aspen, with the ground crisscrossed with tree tops, limbs and stumps, all hidden in knee high grass and ferns. It also had small clearings where the earth was black and sparsely covered with strawberry leaves and wintergreen. Splattered all through the covert were quarter sized whitewash splashings.

We were about 50 yards into the clear-cut when Pixie went on point. We had to pick our way over the fallen timber to get to her. I wanted John to take the shot as I attempted another picture. I was moving and trying to adjust the lighting of the camera at the same time. I would have been fine too, if it weren't for one tiny sapling. I stepped on it to mash it down out of my path. With blinding speed it slipped from beneath my boot and smacked me on the left ear. It was strange that I hadn't noticed how cold my ear was until that very moment. Instant pain and agony. I grabbed the throbbing ear and lurched forward a step catching my foot on a limb hidden by the grass. My lunging hulk broke the limb and crashed down through some rotten sticks with the other foot.

John Jezioro moves in on a woodcock point where Pixie has the bird pinned.

John, Pixie, the woodcock and I were all moving in different directions at the same time. All but me were wondering what it was that was crashing through the covert with such tremendous force. In an instant, what had been a picture of peace, beauty and tranquillity suitable for framing was now a chaotic blur of flashing color, cracking branches, a jingling bell and twittering wings.

Once John realized he was not in danger of being trampled by a displaced water buffalo he directed his attention to the fleeting woodcock. True to its reputation, this bird spiraled up and then leveled off. John's charge of 9's centered the bird and in a few seconds Pixie was standing before us with another large female in her mouth.

With two beautiful woodcock in less than 30 minutes we took a moment to discuss woodcock and woodcock hunting. We laughed at the earlier antics we encountered, and agreed that it all made the day that much more memorable. We also agreed that all who hunt the little timberdoodle have walked in our footsteps before, and live only for the opportunity to get back into the thick of things.

CHAPTER 10

TRADITIONAL GROUSE HUNTING IN THE LAKE STATES IN JEOPARDY

Jack Barnett and I made our first grouse hunt to the Lake States in 1970. We were pioneers from our area; very few, if any, had ventured that far from our home coverts just to hunt grouse. We had good hunting at home during that time, but it was the idea of even better hunting and the call of the North Country that pulled us to Minnesota.

During those early years we had great difficulty finding small game, nonresident license in the little towns of he grouse woods. Once you left the pheasant country, there didn't seem to be any reason to carry small game license for the nonresident. We couldn't convince people back then that we had come over a thousand miles to hunt grouse. As we traveled back and forth in the small towns of Minnesota, and Michigan's Upper Peninsula, we became the talk of the town. We became known as those damn fools who had come all that way just to hunt pats, and with dogs no less.

It was during those early years that we got our first taste of road hunting for grouse. I didn't like it then, and like it less today. When time passed by Michigan's Upper Peninsula, it left behind hundreds of small cabins that could be rented by the fisherman and hunter. These were excellent places for the grouse hunter with dogs. Out of the way and off the highway, hunters and dogs were welcomed. We were at one such small settlement in northern Michigan when we first met the road hunters.

As we checked in, we asked Johnson if there were any other grouse hunters staying with him at the time. He said that the regular gang from Chicago was there just like they had been for past 10 years. It just so happened that they had the cabin next to ours. Early next morning, Jan Riffe and I were up feeding and watering Sally; we only had one dog back then. As we packed our lunch, gathered shells, rain gear and guns, the then. As we packed our lunch, gathered shells, rain gear and guns, the same thing was happening in the next cabin where the fellows from Chicago were staying. We looked for their dog, wanting to see if they had a setter, Brittany or pointer. We didn't see one and assumed they had him kenneled somewhere.

As we talked to them for a moment in the parking lot I was a little embarrassed. I didn't realize how ragged we looked compared to them. I had seen hunters dressed like them before but only on the cover of Orvis or L.L. Bean. Well-tailored and perfectly creased brush pants, Pendelton wool shirts with not a pick or tear, Bass bird hunter boots clean and polished. Their lunches were in matching leather bags and their hunting buggy was a great, long four-door Cadillac.

As they pulled out, Jan and I stood there looking at each other. We too had brush pants and wool shirts. Mine were torn and shredded and his so worn they looked like they were growing hair. Our boots still had the mud caked on from the last hunt. Our lunches were in paper bags. We figured we were out-classed, but we knew from the bottom of our hearts that we had as good a grouse dog as they did and we knew there were no humans who ever hunted harder or loved grouse hunting more.

When we returned after dark our neighbors were already there, again, clean, neat, with drinks in hand and having a great time and a great string of birds hanging on their porch. We too had taken a limit of birds. During those early years it seemed our day was measured by how many birds we took. Thank goodness things have changed. That evening we showed the wear and tear of the tag alder tangles.

This went on for three days, and then on the fourth day our paths crossed. We were coming down an old gravel road, moving to our last covert for the day, when we rounded a curve and saw the Cadillac sitting cross ways in the road. We slowed and saw a long gun barrel come out of the right rear window. Just before the shot I saw a grouse along the edge of the road getting gravel. He never knew he was being hunted.

The shooter, I won't call him a hunter, must have been using duck loads and a full choked gun as it blew the grouse about three feet on down the road. The shooter got out to get his bird and I walked up to the car. I didn't really know what to say so I just asked how they did that day. "Good day, this one gives us all our limit." "Have you been hunting in this area all day," I asked. "Oh no," came the reply. "We have driven about 125 miles today, all the way up the lake shore and back."

I couldn't stand it any longer and asked about their dog. We don't have a dog, one of them laughed. Do you ever lose a bird when you knock one

The changing face of grouse hunting in the Lake States, the ATV. This vehicle may become the scourge of the coverts.

down in a thicket. They laughed again and pointed out that it was hard to lose one in the road.

They seemed eager to talk about their hunting technique, so I kept up the questions. It turned out that they got up in the morning, put on their well tailored outfits, got in the Cadillac and drove every back road they could find, never getting out except to retrieve a grouse they had murdered along the road. Now don't get me wrong, we have road hunters at home but they are deer hunters. The grouse hunters were men with strong legs, lungs and hearts who could walk the mountains all day just to get a fair shot or two at a grouse.

We were guests in this country, so I didn't say anything. I have no problems with how a man hunts if it is legal and fair for the game. What I consider fair and sporting may be only an opinion but what they were doing seemed very wrong. We finished out the week but after that day there wasn't much pleasant conversation between that group and Jan and I. I kept feeling I should say something, but Jan said it might be best if I didn't. As they packed up to go home the last afternoon I couldn't hold it any longer.

I didn't want a major altercation but I wanted to make a point. I walked up to the hunt master and politely asked, "How many grouse do you get per gallon with your Cadillac?" He looked befuddled and I walked away feeling I had made a point. Jan said they had no idea what the point was.

We have hunted the Lake States now for 26 years and in 1992 ran into a new blight in the grouse coverts. The old time road hunters stuck to the main gravel roads. You never saw them on the trails or logging roads. Things have changed drastically, and in many areas it is getting worse by the season.

The ATV, four wheeler, three wheeler and similar machines are great inventions if used for what they were intended. But man, being the imaginative scoundrel that he is, has taken their use to another dimension. They have now become the mainstay of the grouse murderer. It is well documented that grouse in the Lake States gravitate to the clearings and edges of roads that break up the forest cover. It is here they are most vulnerable to the road hunter. The encounter we had with the road shooters in 1970 was the exception. The introduction of the ATV into grouse country is now a major threat to the tradition of grouse hunting as we have known it.

We were on a ten day trip in the Superior National Forest hunting some of the coverts around Ely and Crane Lake. A friend of ours had been bear hunting in this country in September and told us of the large numbers of grouse he had seen while going back and forth to his bear stand. This sounded like the place for us to be with our dogs the first week of October.

We arrived in Crane Lake on October 5th. As we pulled into our cabin, a group of six grouse hunters from Texas were just finishing the day and feeding their dogs. We tried to talk to them but they seemed disgruntled and upset. Were there no birds in the country, was it too hot, too dry or too many hunters, we inquired. One of the fellows said we would soon see what the problem was, about daylight the next morning. He went on to say there were a few birds but that there were hordes of three wheelers and four wheelers cruising every road, lane, path and clearing. They left telling the resort owner that they would not be back again until something was done about the shameless slaughter of so may grouse along the roads. He went on to say they had enough and were pulling out to return to Michigan to finish out their vacation hunt.

Knowing that Texans have a reputation of sometimes stretching the truth, we dismissed their story and turned in. The next morning we were awakened by the sound of a motorcross race. Looking out the window I saw six three and four wheelers going by the cabin, convoy style. On the back of each was an elaborate gun case that made easy and quick access possible, and a small ice chest. What was happening didn't really sink in until we had gathered up the dogs and headed for the coverts.

Rounding a bend in the road we almost ran over them. There were two on each side of the road peering so intently into the edge of the cover along the road that they had no idea we were there. We followed along for about 30 yards, looking for a chance to pass, when one of the fellows stopped and whipped out his shotgun from the opened end of the case.

There about 30-35 yards ahead of him was a big cock grouse picking gravel at the edge of the road. In one smooth motion he opened the single barrel, dropped in a shell, mounted and shot. At the crack of the gun the grouse flattened in a cloud of dust. The shell popped out of the gun, he rammed it back into the case and was off up the road towards the grouse. Only then did he see us behind. He slowed, but didn't stop, bent over, on the still moving four wheeler, and swooped up the lifeless grouse. He motioned to his buddies who turned and then roared on down the road, still two abreast. We sped up and they did too. It was obvious that they wanted to stay ahead of us for fear that we might scare a bird from the road, or worse yet shoot one. The first hour of the hunt was ruined and we decided there were other coverts to hunt.

As the week wore on, we discovered that everything that looked like an opening or trail had ATV tracks all over it. The clover, strawberry and other green plants were too much temptation for the birds and the gangs of ATV riders knew it. We began to inquire around and were stunned at what we were hearing. One fellow on a road grader told us he had shot his limit just about every day since the season opened while running the grader. He had two guns in the grader, a shotgun and a .22 rifle. Talking to the cook at one of the resorts we were told that she got her limit several days, before work and in the evenings, with her .410 as she drove the roads near the small town. I guess the icing came when a lady told us that her daughter had killed three with one shot the other day.

I don't care how many grouse a person shoots in fair chase. What concerns me is that the people doing this type hunting see nothing wrong with it. The real problem is that they are professing to the youngsters that this is grouse hunting and this is the accepted way to hunt. As we began to pay close attention to those on the ATV's, we found that they weren't older hunters who might need a little help in getting back into the coverts. Instead, they were young, healthy individuals, many of whom had their small children strapped on back with them. What a lesson in hunting this must be for them.

The coverts belong to all of us, and you are right, it is none of my business. But I hold a special passion for the dogs, the grouse and this thing we call bird hunting. Because of this passion, I can't accept this intrusion and hope those in power will see fit to bring back the great tradition of hunting as many of us feel it was meant to be.

Trappings of The Grouse Hunter
Guns Don't Kill Grouse: Legs Do

A long time ago someone told me that you don't need a special gun to kill grouse, you need good legs. After 35 years of following pointing dogs from the rugged mountain grouse coverts of southern Appalachia to the gentle aspen barrens of Manitoba, I can testify he was correct. He didn't go far enough, though, because on the ends of the good legs required to follow Old Drummer there has to be a pair of pretty solid feet. I have no idea how many hundreds of miles I have walked, and how many tons of weight lifted it would compute into, but I can tell you that I have tried almost every type of boot made. From the bargain store type to the hand-made European climbing boot, I have searched far and wide for the boot best suited to all grouse hunting.

Like the hat or glove that "fits all," there is no one boot for the job! Let me add also that there is no waterproof leather boot. Many good ones will turn water for a while, but drag them through the grouse coverts covered with briers, rocks, snags and ice, and water will eventually come in. Still, the lightweight leather boot, advertised as waterproof, with a stiff midsole and a good vibrum lug outer sole, is the ticket for grouse hunting where the terrain is rough, steep and slick.

Most of the hunting in the eastern grouse range, meaning Appalachia and into New England, is just this type of terrain. We simply don't have the wet covers that are found around the Lake States. Go farther into New England, up into Maine and the Maritime Provinces, and you will encounter country similar to that of the Lake States. Grouse are found in the deep hollows, steep side hills, mountain plateaus and rolling hills through most of their range.

Country like this calls for a boot with a good, tight fit at the ankle to prevent turning an ankle on a side hill, a fairly stiff midsole to prevent rock bruises, and seven to nine inches of leather uppers to protect the legs from all the things that grab, stick, punch and tangle the legs of the grouse hunter. This is in no way an advertisement, but simply information I will pass on to you. After years of trying everything I could find, I have settled on the boot described above made by either Danner or Dunham. They have simply been the best for me. I am sure others have had equal success with other makes but these have served me well.

There you have it on boots for the grouse hunter. I should mention that you don't want them too high. Seven to nine inches seems to work best, but some get along with a ten inch boot. On the higher ones, most hunters will not use the top one or two holes and then will not tie them very tight. While you need support on your ankles, you need flexibility around your lower calf muscle. These are only guidelines based on my 35 years; the choices are yours. Hopefully these guidelines may save you some of the dollars many like myself spent to gain this knowledge and experience.

Shirts, Jackets and Vests

Out of necessity the grouse hunter must wear some sort of shirt for protection and warmth. In most instances this shirt need not be an extremely heavy one. Due to the continuous walking over broken, uneven, rough terrain, the grouse hunter will stay warm. There will be times when the temperature plummets and you will still be out in the covers, and on those days you may need heavier upper wear. If I had to pick one outfit for 90 % of my grouse hunting it would be a turtleneck thermal undershirt and a light, dress type 100% wool shirt. If it gets moderately cold I can still use this outfit and add a vest. Our arms don't get cold under normal hunting conditions. No matter what I am wearing, it will be the 100% wool shirt over the turtleneck. This will be the first two articles of clothing.

After years of trying everything I had read about, I found that the undershirt will draw out any perspiration and the wool shirt will wick it away from my body. The wool will dry fast if caught in a rainstorm, and even if wet will retain warmth better than cotton. I have found that I get overheated more than I do cold when walking through the grouse coverts that I hunt, most of which are in mountainous areas.

Over this shirt I will wear either a light vest or shooting coat; 90% of the time it will be a short, bright orange vest with back game bag and capacity for a few shells on either side. There are too many vests of this type to try and describe any particular type. One requirement is that they be short and carry the game bag high on the back. If you do get a couple of birds, or if you might be carrying a drink or a sandwich, you want them to ride high on the back and off the hips. The weight on the hips can cause fatigue.

If it is cold, or if a cold wind is blowing, I might replace the vest with a short, bright orange shooting type coat, again with a high riding game bag. This type coat also comes in very handy on those days when I might be hunting a particularly rough piece of cover, one that may be laced with multiflora rose bushes or heavy blackberry briers. This type cover can rip a wool shirt to pieces but the shooting coat will turn them.

All sorts of manufacturers produce exactly what we are talking about here. You can take your choice of fancy or plain. I have an old 40X shooting coat that must have thousands of miles on it but it is very serviceable today, some 25 years after I purchased it. The briers have worn holes in the pockets but the rest is good.

While the outerwear should be roomy and comfortable it should allow freedom. Some of the clothes I see advertised as hunting clothes look more like they are to be worn to the bank. There is nothing at all wrong with style, but it should come second to comfort and freedom of movement.

I remember a close friend of mine showing up one morning with his new hunting pants. He quickly showed me how well tailored they were and how well they fit. I asked him how he got them on over his feet and he smiled as he showed me the zippers in the bottom of the pants legs. I told him I thought they were too tight but he was the one who had to wear them.

Not long after we entered the covert, the walking got a little rough. I noticed the fellow laboring to get his leg up high enough to forge a little stream and some small rocks. The real trial came when we came to a log over the old road we were on. I walked up to the log and stepped over it with little difficulty. I knew what was coming next. My well dressed hunting buddy walked to the log, promptly raised his foot to take the log in stride as he normally would and when his foot didn't clear the log he went head first over the log and into the brush along the trail.

As luck would have it, he ran the barrels of his fancy over/under into the litter of the forest floor and came up with it plugged for the first five inches. While he gathered himself up I cut a stick and cleaned the barrels of his gun. We continued the hunt but by the time we got back his legs were worn clean of hair as the tight-fitting, well tailored pants had about done him in. He never wore them again and we still talk and laugh about it today. Point here is that, no matter what you wear, make sure it allows free, natural movement. If you can't step, jump, squat, bend and throw your shotgun into the shooting position with free movement you will not be a successful grouse hunter.

Bird Guns

Bird guns, like bird hunters, are a breed apart. While many guns used for waterfowl are heavy, stiff and numb, not so for the bird gun. The good ones are light, well balanced, imparting a feeling of being alive, acting as an extension of the gunner's finger as he or she points at a flying bird. From that point on, pride of ownership can dictate choice.

Let me say there is a difference; a well balanced gun, of proper dimensions, fitted to your stature and properly bored for the birds you hunt will make you a better wing shot. Pick a stationary target. Hold the gun as you do when anticipating the flush of a bird while your eyes are fixed on the target some 25 yards away. Throw the gun to your shoulder and the target should be sitting right on top of the bead. If you have to adjust your head, the gun doesn't fit.

Forget all you have read about the target sitting high above the bead. This notion that the gun should shoot high was a carryover from shooting driven birds in Europe, and may also apply to the trap shooter. If your gun shoots high you will shoot high on grouse, woodcock, and definitely on quail that offer many straight away flights while raising very little vertically.

Since you will be doing a lot more carrying than shooting, weight becomes a factor. As I have said before, there is no reason to carry a 7 1/2 pound gun when a 5 3/4 to 6 pound gun will do the same thing. While walking across North America I have no need for anything bigger than a 20 gauge. This is not to say that the 20 is as ballistically efficient as the 12, but what you give up may not be as much as you think.

Jim Hammill, Michigan biologist, friend and avid grouse and woodcock hunter, says that the only difference he could see between the 20 gauge and the 12 gauge was that the 12 might have one or two more birds in a box of shells.

I find that if I am on them I can kill them with the 20 or 28 just as I can with the 16 or 12. A great increase of the efficiency of the 20's and 28's is the use of small, hard shot. A dense pattern is the key.

In the 20's I like an ounce of 8's. In the 28 I prefer 8's, and even 9's, during early season when woodcock and grouse are in the same coverts. If after ringnecks, I switch to 6's as the pheasant is a big, tough bird that will run unbelievable distances with only a broken wing.

In chokes I use skeet #1 in the first barrel and either skeet #2 or imp. cyl., for grouse and woodcock. On quail I have found that I get more dead-in-the-air, bounce-on-the-ground kills with Imp. cyl. in the first barrel and Mod. in the second.

Type of action is a mater of choice. I have shot them all, and for me, no guns balance, point, are more of a joy to carry, and shoot than quality side by sides or over and unders. Again, this is what I have found, and there are many out there who would shoot nothing other than an old model 12, or maybe a light 1100 or even a super-light Franchi 20 gauge. One thing you will find in common among them is that the gun fits.

I will have to say that I have also seen the world's worst possible grouse gun. My friend Dave Marshall is the proud owner of it. Now, Dave could buy about any gun he wanted within reason. His choice is simply based on his idea of using one gun for all of the hunting he does. Dave is a true outdoorsman, hunter, fisherman and lover of nature. He hunts deer, rabbits, squirrels, bear, groundhogs, ducks, geese and grouse with a Savage O/U. It is a 20 gauge full choke over .222 single shot, hammer gun. The hammer has a 10 pound pull to cock it and the trigger has a ten pound pull to fire it. Different strokes, folks!!

Vacant Runs and Empty Collars

I struggled for an ending, and Pixie gave it to me last week. Good-by old friend, may we meet again!

As I drove toward the vet's office, different emotions swept over me in ever increasing black waves of despair. First it was self pity, as I questioned why this had happened just seven days before my birthday. Then anger, as I asked, no one in particular, what Pixie had done to deserve such a plight after only eight years. And then sadness, as that song about John, Bobby and Martin kept echoing in my head. I remember thinking that maybe they were right, maybe the good do die young.

As I neared the vet's driveway, feelings of despair started swelling up again, along with an ache in the pit of my stomach. I kept hoping that the door would open and the doctor would greet me with a wide smile on his face and say that a second exam had revealed the problem to be a minor one easily cured. I pictured him greeting me with a "it wasn't as nearly as bad as we thought." I had agreed that if the doctor's fears proved true, Pixie would go peacefully and painlessly to sleep.

I wanted to run up to the door and shout "I changed my mind," but I knew the die was cast months ago when the first abnormal tumor was removed. Since that first one, we had three more removed, but they just kept coming in greater numbers and with more frequency.

When I opened the door, Dr. Ridenhour's eyes met mine for a brief moment and then he looked away. I knew it was over and my knees seemed a little wobbly. But even then, the reality hadn't sunk in. Only when he laid the cold, black plastic bag across my outstretched arms did the steel hammer of finality finally strike me. There was really nothing to say, and all I could do was turn and walk to the truck with the limp bundle draped over both my arms.

Carefully placing her in the back of the truck, I started the long silent trip home. As I drove along, I remember thinking how lifeless that bundle seemed. There was no wiggling, no whimpering, no soft warm ears or whippy tail. Instead, only the inanimate lump where a good friend had been.

Many of our readers knew Pixie by name, and several by reputation. Still others were lucky to see her in action, Together, Jack Barnett, Jan Riffe, George Burroughs, myself and countless readers followed along over the past eight years as Pixie found bird after bird for the waiting guns. As a tight-knit little group, we walked along after her from the quail fields of Georgia up through the grouse and woodcock coverts of the Lake States and on out over the high plains of Montana.

Pixie came to us as a gift from my friend and mentor, George Burroughs, eight years ago, and from that day to her last she was my dog. She would hunt in front of others in my party, but only long enough to sweep by on her way to her master. I can still see her suspended two feet off the ground, wedged into a 4X4 woven wire fence when she realized we were separated. Unknown to her, I had crossed the fence as we walked the quail fields of Jefferson County. When she found herself separated on Vance's side, she panicked and drove her head and shoulders into the fence, only to become stuck. We freed her with no ill effects and only the pleasant memory of a dog wanting to be with her master.

As Pixie matured, she became our "show dog." She showed many hunters and writers of limited experience that English pointers are like people and should not be stereotyped. She proved that not all pointers are hard headed, independent, arrogant, self hunters that have no place in the close quarters of the grouse and woodcock coverts. She showed that not all pointers blink thick cover or retreat from cold, harsh weather.

Contrary to all this, she showed she was a loyal, trusting, devoted dog whose only purpose in life was to find birds in front of her master and, to do so, she would until she dropped. As more and more hunters were privileged to walk behind her, the reputation was reinforced. Without a doubt, Pixie was the easiest handling bird dog we have ever seen. In fact, there was no handling, you simply went hunting, speaking only to praise her or to send her into some little pocket of cover you wanted her to check out.

While I profess to be her best people friend, I have to admit that her true best friend was our English setter Tomba. Pixie and Tomba were the best working team of bird dogs I have seen. Prime specimens of their respective breeds, they complemented each other with beauty, grace and stamina as they flowed through the black thickets or across the golden stubble. Ed Herzog, and old bird hunter I met in Montana a few years ago, summed it up as he ran his hands over the perfectly chiseled heads of both dogs. "Setters and pointers like Tomba and Pixie, man, it just doesn't get any better."

All these thoughts were racing around in my head and, before I realized it, I was at the end of our field. I will lay her here at the edge of the pines, where the grouse cross the old tram road. There will be sun and shade here in this corner of classic grouse cover. She will be close enough to the house to know we are still there, but far enough away not to be disturbed. There will be noise in the field as we work with her son and daughter, Stoney and Tinker. She will be able to watch as they develop and carry on the great legacy she left with us. They have already made her proud and I am glad she got to see them, as all parents should live long enough to know their children have succeeded.

I don't know if there is a heaven for dogs, but if there is, she will already be there. If Hale-Bopp is truly the Christmas Star of 2,000 years ago, maybe it is showing her the way home as its fading light falls across her grave. Heaven for Pixie would be endless horizons filled with little meandering trails laced with clover and shaded with hawthorn crowned by wild grapevines. It would be the endless milo fields of Kansas and the wheat fields of Montana that run over the horizon, where she races from bird to bird, and when she looks back she will see the smiling faces of Beverly and I. Resting my foot on the shovel, I stop for a moment and think of this picture of what heaven might be for Pixie; I then realize it would be heaven for me also if I could add my family to the picture.

Pixie was the easiest handling grouse dog we ever hunted behind.

I have laid her to rest now, and when the last stone is placed I think of what I should put on it. Then I realize the greatest tribute I can pay her is to say "Pixie was a grouse dog!"

The inscription is finished and I realize how quiet it is as I ease over and sit down on the log where the bird rests and drums on pretty days. A cool breeze comes up from the dark, damp hollow below and sends a chill over me, letting me know the sun is gone.

My thoughts change as I pull up the collar of my jacket and I realize how short a dog's life is in relation to a man's. Dogs' lives are like chapters in the life of a hunter. I know that each of the dogs I have raised and buried over the years have coincided with chapters in my own life. Sitting here with that thought in my mind, I stir the leaves at my feet with a little stick. I also think that it is a month early for my spring allergies to hit me, but my eyes are watering and my nose is stopped up a little, and I rationalize that it must be the piercing night air.

It is time to go now, and as I turn to walk back to the truck I have two last thoughts. "Good-by old friend," and "I wonder how many chapters the Good Lord has put in my Book?"

The Bird Hunter

I chance upon a stranger, in a high mountain glade. "Dear sir," I ask, " can you help me with a sighting I recently made?"

You seem to be a local in this mountain setting so bright, possibly you too have shared this sight?

I had paused in the glade there, when the tinkle of a soft sleigh bell drew my stare.

As I watched a shadow, tall and lean, moved through the trees. Quickly, softly and silently it moved across the covert, "no wait, not one shadow but three!"

Colors flash as the three seemed to melt together only to again scatter, but never far apart. Browns and reds and orange cloak the shadow of the tall, thin one, while the small ones are white and black, tan and ticked.

They are here, there and everywhere, gone and back again. Grace and beauty in motion, so effortlessly do they flow.

But wait, something has gone awry, the small ones are frozen in time, in space in motion and the sleigh bells have fallen deathly silent.

I want to yell out, "is everything all right?," but wait, the tall one, he is now coming into sight. He floats, he ducks, dodges and bends as he threads his way through the thicket so tight.

Now a brown swirl in the leaves and a roar off through the trees, then thunder, from the tall one I think. What happened? The small ones now, they scamper and search. Now one has the brown swirl from the leaves and rushes back to the tall one who is waiting on his knees.

I see him better now as the tatters from his clothes flap in the breeze and the sleigh bells again drift through the trees.

I watched as keenly as I might, but in a minute the forest swallowed them up and they drifted from my sight.

Dear stranger, if you please, can you help me, what was this sight among the distant trees? The tall one with the stick of thunder, the small ones who were every tangle under.

What were they that moved so gracefully and quietly across the forest floor and distant bogs?

"That sir, was THE BIRDHUNTER, and HIS DOGS!!

Frank Jezioro 11-95